How To

MASTER THE UNIVERSE

Personal and Professional Life-Skills Guide

How To

MASTER THE UNIVERSE

Personal and Professional Life-Skills Guide

Tad Bogdan

Copyright © 2023 by Tad Bogdan

All rights reserved. No part of this book may be reproduced in any form or by any electronic or mechanical means, including information storage and retrieval systems, without permission in writing from the publisher except by a reviewer who may quote brief passages in a review.

ISBN 979-8375772622

Paperback Edition 2 (Rev. 5)
Printed by Amazon.com.
Front cover design by Vivienne Tran

Published by Tad Bogdan
www.tadbogdan.com

Disclaimers: The material in this publication is of the nature of general comment only and neither purports nor intends to be advice. Readers should not act on the basis of any matter in this publication without considering (and if appropriate taking) professional advice with due regard to their own particular circumstances. The author and publisher expressly disclaim all and any liability to any person, whether purchaser of this publication or not, in respect of anything and of the consequences of anything done or omitted to be done by any such person in reliance, whether in whole or part, upon the whole or part of the contents of this publication.

Certain data and quotes have been obtained from third-party sources or subject to translations, and neither the author nor publisher warrants the authenticity or accuracy of the third-party data or quotes.

How to MASTER THE UNIVERSE:
Personal and Professional Life-Skills Guide

Endorsements

"Great read! . . . I've never heard it articulated or formalized in this manner. It's interesting to see it explained in a different light and in a more methodical way, especially defining people/things as their own 'universe'."
    Henry Tran - Principal Engineer, SpaceX

"This book is for all ages — your intention of 20 somethings is spot on and we also all know older people who can benefit from this wisdom"
    Donna Carroll - CEO, Alan Carroll & Assoc. (corporate training company)

"What an accomplishment! Your book is just jam-packed with value, so much interesting information, so much priceless, strategic advice, such a broad range of subjects."
    Joshua Hornick - Business Coach

". . . what I find interesting is the "Master the Universe Formula." I feel as if it's a concrete way to find one's way in the real world. I also enjoy seeing the personal anecdotes and quotes sprinkled throughout the book. I would recommend it to young teens!"
    Matthew Dam - Teenage College Student

"Your book is amazing. It matches with the latest findings in quantum mechanics, which Buddhists have been seeking for centuries. The second half is really eye-opening . . ."
    Chihiro Suematsu - Professor, Kyoto University, Graduate School of Management and Stanford University Lecturer

"Tad has the real-life sales, marketing, and leadership experience to provide credibility to the techniques he discusses in the business section of his book. He was a trailblazer at Sun Microsystems, where he started the company's business in nine countries, negotiated one of our largest technology licensing deals, and launched a product that has been licensed to run on tens of billions of chip cards and smartphones. He also demonstrated an early passion for human development when he built and managed the first Sun Field Training organization."
    Scott McNealy - Founder, and CEO of Sun Microsystems, Inc.

How To MASTER THE UNIVERSE:
Personal and Professional Life-Skills Guide

Amazon Reviews

"If you are passionately curious about living your life to the max, I highly recommend reading and learning from this book."

"Great book. It helped me with simple instructions in solving many issues in life from simple to complex. It presents 3 steps to solving life's challenges. It did this clearly, succinctly, and by using examples, charts, anecdotes. This is often done with humor and very relevant quotes. It reads easily. Everyone can use all or parts of the book as a guide to help them master the Universe. A great tool for life."

"Wonderful book full of stories, insights, illuminating quotes and a powerful life changing formula which when applied transforms your unconscious, automatic decision-making process to a state of awareness that allows you to consciously choose the best course of action to take regardless of the life situation you are facing. You become the ruler of your actions and thus...the Master of Your Universe. Everyone, young and old, can benefit from the wisdom that lies within its pages."

"The author deftly touches on numerous approaches to growing and mastering one's mind, body, and spirit - and leveraging his unifying Center of The Universe principle for a more enhanced, mindful, and meaningful being. Regardless of one's age or where one is on their journey toward self-mastery, there's something for everyone in "How to Master the Universe.""

"There are many, many good ideas in this book. I think of the book as situational. Pull it out when you run into something or want to try something new. I especially appreciate the author's work to tie quotes of sages to topics he is addressing."

Topics

INTRODUCTION 1

I. THE CENTER OF THE UNIVERSE 7
    Master The Universe Formula 8
    Your Operating System.. 18
    Thinking Skills.. 22
    The Wisdom Way 29
    Habits and Repetition.. 32
    Memory Skills.. 37
    Space and Timing 38
    Balance... 40

II. MASTERING YOUR UNIVERSE 43
    Maslow's Pyramid 45
    Mindfulness 47
    Your Body.. 51
    Breathing Skills... 53
    Fuel 58
    Sleep 60
    Mantras 62
    Meditation.. 63
    Exercise.. 65
    Behavioral Modification Skills 68
    NLP & NAC Skills 74
    Mind over Matter 77
    Uniqueness... 78
    Personal Mastery... 79

III. MASTERING OTHER UNIVERSES ... 83
    Diversity.. 84
    Relationships... 87
    Rapport Skills 88
    Smiling... 96
    Probing & Listening Skills... 97

Restraint	100
Interactive Behavioral Modification	103
Influencing with NLP	105
Setting Expectations	106
Conflicts	107
Winning	111
Judgmentalism	114
Forgiveness	116
Focus	117
The Power of Persuasion	118

IV. THE COSMOS 121

Cosmic Balance	123

V. MASTERING OUTCOMES 125

Life	125
Reincarnation	126
Virtue	129
Attitude	131
Rules	134
Self-determination	136
Mistakes	137
Karma	140
Gratitude	145
Choices	148
Success: Money vs. Karma	149
Next	155

ADDENDUM: BUSINESS & PROFESSIONAL SKILLS 161

Money & Profit	162
Honest Capitalism	165
Business	166
Leaders, Managers, and Bullies	168

Leadership Skills 172
Coaching Skills 174
Public Speaking Skills 177
Negotiation Skills 183
Sales Skills 187
Marketing Skills 197
Added Value 204

AFTERWORD 207

ACKNOWLEDGEMENTS 209

SAMPLE DISCUSSION POINTS 213

RESOURCES 217

ABOUT THE AUTHOR 219

INTRODUCTION

If you had a choice, would you rather be smarter — or be able to improve your powers of persuasion? Would you rather be right — or would you rather win? Do you want to be good — or to be lucky? Do you want to be successful in your personal life — or in your professional life?

You do not have to choose between these options. You can achieve all of the above and more. In fact, mastering one of the choices can help accelerate your success with the others.

The objective of this book is to help you master your personal and professional lives, to accomplish this while enjoying life — and while having a positive impact on the rest of the world.

This book captures a concise synopsis of a broad base of concepts instead of diving too deeply into each topic. The book covers 61 topics. You may already be an expert in some of the topics. Other topics may not be relevant to where you are in this stage of your life journey — while other readers may find them important right now. Many of the topics are the subject of whole books, courses, and even complete fields of study. Some of the concepts are based on scientifically proven principles and others are based on theories that are open to further exploration.

The book is sprinkled with intriguing quotes and anecdotes to help illustrate the concepts. I will include select examples of practical techniques and practices to help you apply the concepts in real-life situations — but to keep it concise, I am leaving a wealth of examples, stories, and exercises open for inclusion in future books and workshops.

This serves as more of a guide and reference book than a story book about the concepts. Story books can be more entertaining the first time you read them but are more difficult to use as reference resources. You can read this book the first time to establish a foundation for the concepts and then return to the book whenever you want a refresher on topics such as thinking, memory, meditation, or breathing techniques, establishing rapport, public speaking, or various professional skills. Topics like these will have much more significance "in the moment" — when you are preparing to engage in the actual activity.

> Guidebooks provide shortcuts to the highlights of locations on a journey — but you should go back to spend more time at a location if you really want to understand and appreciate it.

Whatever works best for you might be different from what works best for others. This is particularly important for health-related concepts which are based on generic studies and theories. Always defer to professional medical advice based on your specific health conditions. We are all unique and alternative concepts and approaches may be more effective for you. You may discover other theories and practices to achieve your objectives — and you are encouraged to pursue more detailed follow-on studies and training in your areas of interest.

Words are just symbols for concepts and objects. A specific word can have different meanings to different people, and different meanings in different situations. Things "are what they are" regardless of what word is used to describe them. It is more important to agree on what we are using a word to represent, than to debate over the meaning of a word. So, definitions are often provided in the book to help clarify what meaning is being applied for a given word in the book.

Several diagrams are also included to help visualize concepts. The diagrams can only be presented in a book in two dimensions, whereas many relationships are more complex and multi-dimensional. Two- and three-

INTRODUCTION

dimensional diagrams and formulas often represent the physical variables of length, width, and height, whereas dimensions can also represent other variables such as time, or multiple data points. Even with a two-dimensional constraint, creating these diagrams helped me clarify some of my thinking around the topics they visualized.

The foundation of the book is based on a basic principle called the **COTU (Center of the Universe) Principle** and the application of **THE FORMULA (Master the Universe Formula).** Consequently, you will notice repetition and reinforcement of these and other concepts as they apply to the various subjects covered in the book.

I wrote this book as if I was providing advice to myself — and I am still learning. It is the book that I wish I had available to me throughout adulthood and the book that I would like to have waiting for me if I happen to be reincarnated. As such, some of the advice extends beyond the topics directly related to the **COTU Principle** and **THE FORMULA**. Many are based on experiences that I have learned over time, and some were gleaned from recent research to create this book. Every one of the topics is a snapshot of key learnings that I have valued over time, and I hope that you find them beneficial as well.

> "I have no special talent. I am only passionately curious."
> Albert Einstein (1879-1955), Theoretical
> Physicist

Section I will introduce the **COTU Principle,** and how **THE FORMULA** can be applied to mastering aspects of your personal life as well as your interactions with other entities — including people, animals, organizations, and the world around us. Universes are constantly evolving, so mastering the Universe will always be a work-in-progress — requiring a process of continuous improvement.

To help appreciate how to use our minds to manage our bodies and behaviors more effectively, this section will provide an overview of how our operating systems and minds operate, how to think more effectively, and the application of repetition, space, and balance.

Section II is focused on mastering your personal Universe. This section starts with an overview of Maslow's Pyramid — which identifies a hierarchy of priorities for the needs that motivate human behavior and continues exploring mindfulness along with principles and practices to achieve a state of relaxed focus. This section includes theories and practices to improve your self-awareness, and personal behavioral modification.

Section III explores techniques for mastering your impact on other Universes. I expand on applications of the personal behavioral modification techniques as they apply to others as well as introducing additional techniques such as rapport building and powers of persuasion.

Section IV explores the bigger picture, or the Cosmos, which incorporates all the Universes in existence and explores how we can improve our relationship with the Cosmos.

In **Section V** sums up with principles and philosophies to achieve success in your life such as attitude, rules, karma, and your control over the choices you make. This is the formal conclusion of the book for many readers.

The **Addendum: Business and Professional Skills** applies the **COTU Principle** and **THE FORMULA** towards success in your professional life. This is included as an addendum because there is a heavy emphasis on business applications, which may not be of interest to everyone. Some of the topics such as Money & Profit, Leadership and Public Speaking could be relevant to you though, even if you are not engaged in a business profession.

Feel free to skip around to sections that are a short-term priority for you. For example, if you have an impending public speaking engagement, skip to the section on Public Speaking, which will lead you back to reviewing the section on Breathing.

INTRODUCTION

"God, grant me the serenity to accept the things that I cannot change, the courage to change the things I can, and the wisdom to know the difference."
Rev. Reinhold Niebuhr (1892 – 1971),
American Theologian

The title of this book is *How to MASTER THE UNIVERSE,* and the process to master the universe follows a pathway called **The Wisdom Way**.

How To MASTER THE UNIVERSE
Personal and Professional Life-Skills Guide

I. THE CENTER OF THE UNIVERSE

You are the **Center of the Universe** — the Center of your Universe.

Every other entity is the **Center of their Universe** too — driven by their own survival and success.

Each one of us considers ourselves as "the" **Center of the Universe**. We can each Master our own Universe. We can also master our relationship with other Universes. The first step towards mastering the universe is to define the term "Universe."

> **Universe:** a world or sphere in which something exists or prevails.
> *Dictionary.com*

Since Universes are constantly changing and evolving, the process of mastering a Universe will always be a work-in-progress. The guiding principle of this book is that each entity is the Center of its own Universe. I am calling this the **COTU (Center of the Universe) Principle**.

> **COTU Principle:** Every entity is the Center of its own Universe and is motivated by its own survival and success.

The **COTU Principle** applies to every human, animal, or other conscious entity — even a grasshopper is the center of its own Universe. The **COTU Principle** also applies to organizations such as religions, governments, and corporations. We are all driven to survive and thrive.

Think about this principle as you sit in a meeting, walk through a crowd, or see people driving cars on the road.

Think about it when you interact with a loved one, a friend, a colleague, a stranger — or even an adversary. Keep reminding yourself that, from their own frames-of-reference, everyone else is the Center of the Universe. By keeping this concept in mind as you navigate through life, you will become more effective at mastering your impact on other Universes — and improve the odds of accomplishing your objectives. This includes mastering your personal, interpersonal, and professional lives.

Master The Universe Formula

Whether you believe that you can Master the Universe, or not — you are correct.

This section introduces a three-step formula for putting **COTU Principle** into action. The same formula applies to mastering your Universe as well as mastering your interactions with other Universes. The **Master the Universe Formula** may sound straightforward, but it takes a concerted effort to apply it consistently. One of the initial challenges towards implementing **THE FORMULA** is within your control — the ability and effort required to think effectively.

Master The Universe Formula
THE FORMULA = OO + RRR + AA

1. **OO** – Determine your Objectives and Options.
2. **RRR** – Consider potential Results, Reactions, and Rewards to determine your course of action.
3. **AA** – Act and Assess.

PRO TIP: Use the condensed acronym **"ORA"** to remember **THE FORMULA**.

I. THE CENTER OF THE UNIVERSE

Step 1: OO - Determine **Objectives & Options.** Objectives are the results you want to accomplish in each situation, whether it only affects mastering your Universe or involves an interaction with another entity's Universe. Ask yourself why you want to accomplish these Objectives and then decide if you want to modify your Objectives. Consider potential Optional actions towards achieving your Objectives. If you do not take the time and effort to think through what you want to accomplish before taking action, you may be surprised by the results. Keep the **COTU Principle** in mind when determining your Objectives and the potential Results of your actions. How does it apply to you and to others affected by your decisions? Think about your Objectives, Options, and potential Results — but be careful not to take so long that you miss the opportunity to Act.

> "Now, in matters of action, the reason directs all things in view of the end."
> Thomas Aquinas (1225-1274), Philosopher and Theologian

Step 2: RRR - Consider **Results, Reactions** and **Rewards** for each option. What is the potential benefit or Reward to you or the other entity? If you were in similar situations in the past, how did you and other parties react? Consider how the dynamics may have changed since the last time you were in a similar situation. Thinking about how you might react is a good start. I will introduce behavioral modification techniques to better understand and train your reactions — and other party's reactions.

Since everyone is different, consider how the other party might react differently than how you would react. The **Mastering Other Universes** Section will explore how people are wired differently — which can vary their Reactions. They are the Center of their Universes, and their Universe includes different experiences and backgrounds than your Universe.

If you want to influence someone else's behavior,

consider whether it is better to ask a question than make a statement. You will often get a better Reaction if you stimulate the other party to go through their own thought process rather than simply stating your opinion.

> The Socratic Method involves asking questions to stimulate someone's thought process rather than simply telling them your conclusion. One of the benefits of this method is that the recipient ends up with a sense of ownership to the answer by having derived the answer with their own mind and brain. They might even come up with a better conclusion than you have thought of — or a conclusion that is more applicable from their frame of reference.

If you have the time, cycle through Steps 1 and 2 multiple times to identify the Action that you think will produce the optimal combination of Results, Reactions and Rewards for you and the other parties involved. For important decisions, you might want to brainstorm through THE FORMULA with a friend, or an advisor for a more objective perspective.

> "Have you ever considered the consequences of your actions?"
> *Mary Shelly's Frankenstein*, 1994 Movie

Step 3: Act and Assess (once you have decided) - The most important step includes selecting the most promising Actions towards achieving your desired Objectives — following through with your selection — and then learning from the experience to accomplish optimal results the next time.

> "If the highest aim of a captain were to preserve his ship, he would keep it in port forever."
> Thomas Aquinas (1225-1274), Philosopher and Theologian

Deciding to avoid or delay an action is also a decision on how to proceed. You should Act when the time is right.

I. THE CENTER OF THE UNIVERSE

Sometimes it is better to wait for a more appropriate time to Act. Decide if refraining from acting or speaking in the moment could yield better results and define you better than with an immediate response.

> "It is not only what we do, but also what we do not do, for which we are accountable."
> Moliere (1622–1673), French Playwright and Actor

Waiting also gives you time to listen, ask questions, observe, and consider potentially more effective actions. The dynamics surrounding the situation can change as well, to afford a more effective time to Act.

Other times, immediate action is more effective than waiting. You do not want to miss your best, or only opportunity to act. When it is time to act, it is often best to Act decisively.

> "Take time to deliberate; but when the time for action arrives, stop thinking and go in."
> Napoleon Bonaparte (1769–1821), French Emperor

After you have Acted (or refrained from Action) and Assessed the results, you can feed them into your learning cycle for the next time you encounter a similar decision. Decide, Act, learn — and move forward.

Examples:
THE FORMULA = OO + RRR + AA

Example A: The Laundry Room Dilemma
When I was young and moved into my first apartment in California, I invited my parents to visit and stay with me. I started my laundry in the laundry room and went on a few errands prior to picking up my parents at the airport at 10 PM. My laundry included my only sheets and towels for my parents

and me to use during their visit. When I returned from my errands shortly after 9 PM, I discovered that the laundry room was locked at 9 PM every night and I was too late to retrieve my laundry.

1. **OO – Determine your Objectives and Options.** My objective was to have clean sheets available for my parents when they arrived.
    a. One option I considered was to call the security number on the laundry room door to ask them to open the door.
    b. I could try to break the door or glass to get to my laundry.
    c. Another option that I thought up was calling the security office a few minutes later and telling them that a suspicious-looking person was hanging around the laundry room. And then asking the security guard to unlock the door for me when he arrived.
2. **RRR – Consider potential Results, Reactions, and Rewards to determine your course of action.**
    a. I tested option a. by calling the security number and they said that they only respond to emergencies and this situation did not qualify.
    b. I did not really consider the option of breaking the door or glass for ethical reasons. Even if I had tried this option, if caught, the condo management's reaction would be very negative, potentially resulting in damage fees and even criminal charges.
    c. The result that I wanted was to explain the situation to the security guard and hope that he would react with sympathy — and let me in the room and collect my

laundry. He would be rewarded with the satisfaction of helping a fellow human being and I would be rewarded with happy parents. I thought that I was being clever, but another potential reaction to this option could be for the security guard to call the police or pull out a weapon when approaching the laundry room. This option could have ended with a punishment rather than a reward.

3. **AA – Act and Assess**. I decided to proceed with option c. reporting a suspicious person near the laundry room and waiting for the security guard. I used a subset of the TENS technique covered in the Rapport section of the book when he arrived. Fortunately, the security guard was nice and let me retrieve my laundry. After assessing the decision, I concluded that I took an unnecessary risk. A better option would have been to go to one of the stores that was open later to purchase some new sheets. I would eventually need additional sheets anyways and I could have avoided the risk involved with my choice. My learning from this was to take the time to think through additional options before acting.

Example B: Reunion Penthouse Suite
My ten-year high school reunion was held over a weekend at the Don Cesar Hotel, an iconic, historic, luxury hotel on St. Petersburg Beach, Florida. I was flying in from California and had reserved and pre-paid for a private hotel room several months in advance for this special occasion. When I arrived, the desk clerk informed me that the standard rooms were sold out and I would be assigned a living room

lock-off from a suite with a fold-out-couch for my bed.
1. **OO – Determine your Objectives and Options.** My objectives were to have a nice room to myself at the reunion hotel with a real bed to sleep on.
    a. One option was to accept my fate and make the best of the weekend with the assigned room.
    b. A reflexive option was to get upset at the clerk and try to fight for a better room.
    c. Another option was to book a standard room at a neighboring hotel.
    d. The final option I considered was to think through the respective reactions, rewards, and results — and to problem solve with the clerk and hotel for an alternate win-win solution.
2. **RRR – Consider potential Results, Reactions, and Rewards to determine your course of action.**
    a. Simply accepting my fate would have been unrewarding. It would not have delivered the results I hoped for and would have had a disappointing reaction that would have shadowed the whole weekend. On the other hand, the clerk would have been happily rewarded with an easy resolution.
    b. If I had gotten mad and argued with the clerk, the clerk might have had a defensive reaction and argued back. I might have even been kicked out of the hotel, ruining the whole reunion weekend ending with an extremely unrewarding lose-lose resolution.
    c. Booking a room at a neighboring hotel would have probably been less rewarding

I. THE CENTER OF THE UNIVERSE

to me than option a. — albeit rewarding to the clerk.

d. Problem solving with the clerk and hotel management could be accomplished by respecting their rules and limitations, positively acknowledging their support in a way that they would feel rewarded, explaining my perspective, and exploring options together.

3. **AA – Act and Assess.** I used a subset of the TENS technique covered in the Rapport section of the book and calmly told the clerk that I respected the hotel's dilemma — but I had booked and pre-paid for my room months in advance of many of the guests who had checked in earlier that day. One option that I suggested would be to move one of those guests into the lock-off room and giving me the resulting standard room that I had already paid for. The clerk did not have the authority to do this so I politely asked if we could bring in the manager to explore other options that he might be able to approve. I again applied the TENS technique with the manager. He said that there was a penthouse suite available, but it would cost considerably more than the room I paid for. It was late in the day, and I suggested that they were losing even a standard fee for the penthouse suite if it was still available. If they let me have the room at a standard rate, everyone would be very happy. Assessment – joint problem solving worked. The hotel staff took very good care of me, and I ended up with a penthouse suite at a standard rate for a very satisfying reunion weekend.

Note: I have been rewarded with complementary upgrades to penthouses, presidential suites, and first-class airplane seats many times by establishing rapport, applying THE FORMULA, and being empathetic for the other person's universe.

Example C: Road Rage Reduction
Have you ever been in a situation when another driver cuts you off in traffic? How do you react?
1. **OO** – Determine your Objectives and Options. Was your objective to arrive at your destination safely and efficiently?
    a. A reflexive option is to get angry, yell or make obscene gestures to the other driver.
    b. You could cut through the traffic to try to get ahead over the other driver and cut them off.
    c. You could also consider the other driver's universe and chose not to react. Or to react with a friendly smile, peace sign, or wave. They might be rushing for a medical emergency, running late for a life-changing interview or wedding — or maybe they are just being a jerk.
2. **RRR – Consider potential Results, Reactions, and Rewards to determine your course of action.**
    a. If you get angry, yell, or make obscene gestures to the other driver you risk raising your blood pressure and getting into a bad mood. The other driver might react by slamming on their brakes or doing something even more violent like using a gun — putting you into danger and slowing you down even further.

I. THE CENTER OF THE UNIVERSE

    b. This could produce the same results as option a. and put you in danger of recking into another car.
    c. With this option, you can maintain your good attitude and add to your Karma Pool (discussed later) — traveling safely and with minimal impact on your arrival time.
3. **AA – Act and Assess. I will leave this for your consideration.**

Some people already apply the steps of **THE FORMULA** — and many others simply assume that they do without taking the time to think through the three steps. The section on **Thinking** studies on how our brains typically process challenging situations and approaches to improve our attention to **THE FORMULA**. It takes focus and repetition to ingrain this practice into your everyday life and apply **THE FORMULA** successfully.

I think about **THE FORMULA (OO + RRR + AA)** constantly. I am frequently in situations where I can react to a situation reflexively and be correct without achieving ideal Results. I have learned that I achieve much better Results when I take the time to think through **THE FORMULA**. When I forget to think through **THE FORMULA** before responding or when I apply it and do not get the ideal Results, I use it as a learning experience for the future.

Mastery of **THE FORMULA** is an iterative process — it takes time to assess the Results of your Actions. If your Actions do not generate desired outcomes or reactions, you can adjust accordingly the next time that you are in a similar situation — and it takes focus and effort.

> "You have brains in your head. You have feet in your shoes. You can steer yourself any direction you choose. You're out on your own. And you know what you know. And YOU are the one who'll decide where to go . . ."
> Dr. Seuss (1904 – 1991), Author and Cartoonist

How To MASTER THE UNIVERSE
Personal and Professional Life-Skills Guide

Your Operating System

The first phase of Mastering the Universe is exploring how your mind and brain act compared to how a computer operating system would manage your actions. I will start by discussing how your operating system is structured with the objective of learning how to leverage it to think more effectively in the pursuit of mastering your behavior. You are a combination of physical and non-physical components. Like a computer, you have an operating system that directs and manages your decisions and actions. The operating system in a computer is the master software that interprets the instructions from an application and directs the follow-through of the computer hardware. This similarity is no accident — traditional computer architectures were patterned after the way humans operate. Your operating system enables you to choose how you want to follow through to master your Universe and the other Universes where you interact.

"Knowing yourself is the beginning of all wisdom."
Aristotle (384-322 BC), Greek Philosopher

Human operating systems have parallels to a computer's operating system with the added benefit that we have a capacity for self-determination. But even the ability of self-determination in computers is progressing with the evolution of Artificial Intelligence (AI). Both humans and computers have layers of non-physical elements which interact with physical elements. A software program interacts with another device using a computer operating system, and our souls interact with our bodies using our human operating systems.

There is even a parallel concept to the function of the firmware for a computer. The firmware in a computer is the machine level code that provides direct control of the device's specific hardware. The programming of our brain in our bodies is analogous to the firmware programmed into devices. And our minds can update the programming of our brains to some extent, analogously to the capability to update the firmware programming in some devices.

This metaphor contemplates the existence of a soul that exists beyond the physical limits of our body, and in turn, beyond the limits of the physical world. Since our bodies have a finite life cycle, our souls are the true centers of our respective Universes.

There are conflicting and overlapping definitions for the words Spirit and Soul in various religious dogma — and the concepts are more important than debating which concept applies to which word. I will use the following definitions for the layers of interactions for our operating systems.

> **Soul:** the principle of life, feeling, thought, and action in humans, regarded as a distinct entity separate from the body,
> **Mind:** (in a human or other conscious being) the element, part, substance, or process that reasons, thinks, feels, wills, perceives, judges, etc.
> **Spirit:** the principle of conscious life; the vital principle in humans, animating the body or mediating between body and soul.
> **Brain:** the part of the body's central nervous system enclosed in the cranium of humans, serving to control and coordinate the mental and physical actions.
> **Body:** the corporal, organic physical structure, and material substance of a human.
> *Dictionary.com*

SOUL-BODY MODEL

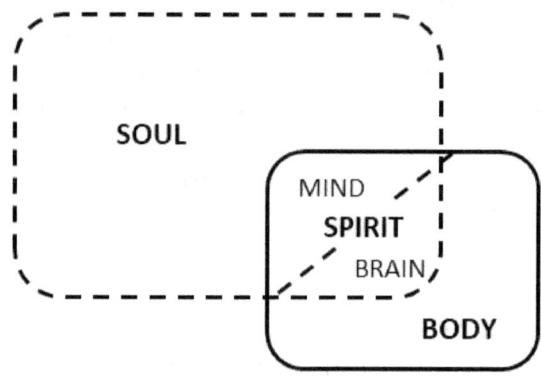

Our souls are the non-physical elements of our beings, and our bodies are temporary, physical extensions of our beings. Our minds are the part of our souls that process inputs and make decisions to be directed to our bodies through our spirits. Just as our minds are subsets of our souls, our brains are subsets of our bodies. Our spirits are where our minds mesh with our brains to channel communications between our souls and bodies. Some cultures and religions also believe that creatures (such as animals and insects) and objects (such as plants, trees, and rocks) have souls too.

Your operating system is what enables you to execute the three steps to **Master the Universe**. First, use your mind to determine your objectives and options. Then consider how you want the other party to react; how you would react, and how the other party might react differently than you. Take actions towards achieving your objectives and assess the results. And finally, assess the results of your actions — and learn from your experiences.

Our bodies have strengths and limitations. They will grow up, grow old and only exist for a finite period of time. We can even replace parts of our body such as certain joints and organs, while continuing our spiritual mind/brain

I. THE CENTER OF THE UNIVERSE

connection to the physical world. When we replace a hip, we still have the same mind and soul.

When your body dies, your soul has finished its lease on your body — so you should try to master your soul's symbiotic relationship with your body while you have the opportunity to experience physical life. Through our bodies, our souls can experience the joys and pains of living in the physical world. This ability is one of the amazing advantages that humans currently have over computers and machines.

Our bodies have traits that have been genetically programmed through thousands of years as the human species has evolved. The physical bodies that we are leasing come with some common physical boundaries, along with individually unique combinations of physical attributes. We also have the fortunate ability, within these boundaries, to re-program some of our body's capabilities and behaviors to maximize its strengths and minimize its weaknesses.

> "The spirit is willing, but the flesh is weak."
> *Bible*, Matthew 26:41, New International Version

The most important step towards Mastering the Universe is making the decision that your mind and soul are the masters of your brain and body. Our bodies are like a machine where our brain is the control room that directs the activities of our bodies — and our minds have the capability to exert management authority over our brain. Your brain is genetically programmed to react and behave in certain ways — but you can use your focused mind power to override and reprogram many of these behaviors. I will expand on this further in the sections on Maslow's Hierarchy of Needs and forms of Behavioral Modification.

> "It is not enough to have a good mind. The main thing is to use it well."
> Rene Descartes (1596–1650), Philosopher and Mathematician

Our operating systems have the dynamic ability to learn from successes and failures and evolve or reprogram our follow-on actions accordingly. One objective of this book is to discuss practical approaches to improve the results of our decisions and achieve a more fulfilling life.

Thinking Skills

"I cannot teach anybody anything. I can only make them think."
Socrates (470–399 BC), Greek Philosopher

You have the power to think more effectively — the power to become smarter — and the power to use your mind to master your brain, your body, and behaviors.

"Thinking is the hardest work there is, which is the probable reason why so few engage in it."
Henry Ford (1863-1947), Founder of Ford Motor Company

Thinking is not really that hard. It is not painful. In fact, thinking can help reduce or avoid pain. It is just that some types of thinking require more effort than others. You just need to decide what type of thinking to apply to a situation, do it — and make a habit of doing it.

"I think, therefore I am."
Rene Descartes (1596–1650), Philosopher, and Mathematician

"I think, I think I am, therefore I am, I think."
"In the Beginning" (1969), by The Moody Blues

"I think, therefore I am"
"Therefore I Am" (2020), by Billie Eilish

I. THE CENTER OF THE UNIVERSE

There are many ways to categorize thinking processes — such as logical thinking, delusional thinking, wishful thinking, and instinctive thinking.

This book will define and divide our thinking processes into Reflexive, Engaged, and Mindful Thinking processes. I will focus on the differences between the Reflexive and Engaged Thinking processes in this section and expand upon Mindful Thinking in the section on Mindfulness.

The Engaged Thinking process is especially useful for applying THE FORMULA (OO + RRR + AA) more effectively.

> In a chess game, the most efficient path to victory is not through making each move as quickly as possible. Success is achieved by taking the time to think through each of your moves. Thinking through the immediate benefits and potential consequences as well as the impact on your long-term and ultimate objective of capturing your opponent's king. Not even pre-touching the piece that you are considering moving to avoid unintended telegraphing of your alternative strategies — unless you consciously want to create a little confusion and misdirection. Then after every move, assessing your opponent's reaction and the impact on your strategy before beginning the process over again for your next move.

Nobel Prize laureate, Daniel Kahneman, studied how the human brain operates and separates our typical thinking processes into two modes, which have been referred to as the System 1 and System 2 — or the Type 1 and Type 2 thinking processes. Dr. Kahneman claims that everyone utilizes one or both processes to varying degrees depending on the situation. These two thinking processes are comparable to what I am calling the Reflexive Thinking and Engaged Thinking processes. I am also adding the Mindful Thinking process to the list.

Thinking Processes:

Reflexive Thinking – The reflexive mode of thinking when you instinctively react to stimuli without stopping to think through alternative actions and consequences.

Engaged Thinking – The analytical mode of thinking when you take the time and effort to think through the alternatives and consequences of your actions.

Mindful Thinking (Mindfulness) – The mode of thinking where you focus on the present moment while freeing your mind from the past, the future, and external distractions.

The Reflexive Thinking process is a quick, easy, and intuitive approach to thinking and problem solving. Reflexive Thinking is only capable of simple relationships. This process is critical in crisis situations where a fast response is essential for your very survival. Your reflexive, default mode which requires the minimal amount of energy from your brain to complete a task.

> "About 43 percent of everyday actions are done repeatedly almost every day in the same context. It's very much like driving. We have this general sense that we're doing things, but it's not driven by an active decision-making process."
> Wendy Wood, USC Psychology Professor

Whereas Reflexive Thinking primarily relies upon your brain, Engaged Thinking uses your mind and brain to focus on a present situation. Mindful Thinking is a mode where you disengage from Reflexive and Engaged Thinking — liberating your mind from the distractions of your brain and body to let thoughts flow naturally from your mind.

The Engaged Thinking process is the operating mode that your mind enters when it is focusing and expending more energy to solve more complex problems. If your Reflexive Thinking process is confused, it creates cognitive strain, and

I. THE CENTER OF THE UNIVERSE

your mind shifts into the Engaged Thinking mode. The Reflexive Thinking Process continuously generates suggestions for your Engaged Thinking mode as well. If the Reflexive Thinking suggestions are endorsed by your Engaged Thinking process — the intuitions are turned into beliefs — and your impulses turn into voluntary actions. In a heightened Engaged Thinking state, your mind starts to check on the judgements we have made in the Reflexive Thinking state of mind before endorsing the judgements. To save energy and operate more effectively, our body typically avoids invoking Engaged Thinking unless we are confronted with an unfamiliar or confusing problem to solve.

> The Reflexive Thinking process leaves you in a state of cognitive ease. A state of more relaxed perception, memory, judgement, and reasoning. It relies on reactive instead of deliberate thinking.

Many of the Reflexive Thinking default reactions are engrained into our brains over centuries of genetic survival programming. Other reactions are invoked by associative memory, programmed through repetition and familiarity during our physical lifetimes. If we did not utilize Reflexive Thinking, we would run the risk of going crazy by overthinking everything and never accomplishing anything. The key is to be aware, and wary of quick decisions, and learn when to revert to the Engaged Thinking process.

> Reflexive Thinking is like making assumptions. Some people say that they never make assumptions. If they never made assumptions, they would never trust that other cars normally stay in their lanes or stop at streetlights. They would be so paranoid that they would never be able to drive or ride down the street to go to the store.

Sometimes our Reflexive Thinking mode's intuitive thinking can be amazingly effective because our subconscious minds are recognizing patterns that our conscious minds might miss. For example, there may be times when you perceive that someone is lying. You may not be sure why, but your subconscious mind has recognized certain behavior differences between when a person is telling the truth or lying, such as eye movements, posture, the pitch, or the rate of speech.

There is also a risk to taking Reflexive Thinking shortcuts which can lead to judgmental errors and hasty decisions. Reflexive Thinking can provide impressions that often turn into your beliefs without your conscious awareness – and familiarity is not easily distinguished from truth. If you restrict your thinking to the Reflexive Thinking process, you will limit your intelligence and ability to **Master the Universe**.

> "Most men seem to live according to sense than reason."
> Thomas Aquinas (1225-1274), Philosopher and Theologian

Conversely, appealing to someone else's Reflexive Thinking can be highly effective towards mastering your interactions with them. Marketing campaigns often associate their products with familiar images to put people into a relaxed state of cognitive ease, whereas statistics, which appeal to Engaged Thinking create cognitive discomfort.

There are actual physiological pathways from your amygdala in your brain for Reflexive and Engaged Thinking. These are the thalamic pathway for Reflexive Thinking and the cortical pathway for Engaged Thinking. The thalamic pathway is twice as fast, but the cortical pathway involves the brain's cortex, where higher cognitive functions take place.

> "Amygdala fire up fight or flight response. Trigger emotional reactions. Your success at survival depends on how you handle the daily torrent of emotions activated by your amygdala.

I. THE CENTER OF THE UNIVERSE

> Survival can depend on the ability to stay calm & focused."
> *The Survivors Club*, By Ben Sherwood (1964-)

Reflexive Thinking oversees impulses whereas Engaged Thinking reigns over self-control and willpower. Consequently, your mastery of the Engaged Thinking process is key to your ability to exercise free will. You can simply let things happen to you, driven by outside forces with your Reflexive Thinking process, or you can take control with your mind by exercising Engaged Thinking. You have a choice — you have the power.

> "Those who know how to think need no teachers."
> Mahatma Gandhi (1869-1948), Indian Civil
> Rights Leader

Training your mind to focus on one thought at a time with Engaged Thinking makes it easier to solve complex problems. You can break down and organize the problem into more manageable components — and then more easily accomplish the tasks on a one-by-one basis.

Focus Process:

1. If your mind starts to wander and multitask — pause.
2. Prioritize tasks and options based on objectives.
3. Put lower priority tasks aside, then focus and be present with the highest priority task.

This is the process you can use to apply **THE FORMULA (OO + RRR + AA)**. Keep in mind that Engaged Thinking requires attention and effort.

> Whereas the brain only takes up 1 to 2 percent of our body mass, it uses approximately 25% of our body's energy.

Intelligence is not only the ability to reason — it is also the ability to find relevant material in memory — and to deploy attention when needed. You can improve your intelligence through self-control, and you can improve self-control through repetition.

If you let your Reflexive Thinking process dictate your decisions and actions, you are giving up control to external stimuli — you are letting other Universes be the master of your Universe. Fortunately, you can override your tendency to rely on Reflexive Thinking — and to be more conscious about when to invoke your Engaged Thinking process. You can monitor the situations where you benefit from Reflexive Thinking and make sure that you own the decision as to when it will be better to rely on Reflexive Thinking or to employ Engaged Thinking.

One exercise to train your mind's ability to break the chain of Reflexive Thinking is to take a mundane daily task and do it differently, such as brushing your teeth with the other hand than you are used to using or showering with your eyes closed.

> My stepson is a scientist who started his own life sciences technology company, I asked him what activity he did most during his day. He said "thinking." He also spent considerable time increasing his knowledge through reading and research.

Being a scientist, he may have had the flexibility and responsibility to make thinking his number one priority, but we all can all carve out some time to think and learn. Try to periodically carve out other distractions and keep our mind focused on one topic at a time.

I. THE CENTER OF THE UNIVERSE

"We cannot solve our problems with the same level of thinking that created them."
Albert Einstein (1879-1955), Theoretical Physicist

There is also a concept called the Extended Mind, where you can expand your thinking and learning process beyond your mind-brain interaction by learning through the rest of your body, your environment, and social interactions. The section on Mindfulness will explore methods to open and engage our Extended Mind thinking processes.

"We all have the power of thought, so what are you lacking? If you have willpower, then you can change anything."
Dalai Lama IV (1940-), Buddhist Spiritual Leader

The Wisdom Way

The **Wisdom Way** is the repetitive process for applying **THE FORMULA** to **Master the Universe**.

There is a difference between knowledge and wisdom. Knowledge involves the storage and recall of information. Wisdom involves making judgements about the information — and how you decide to act upon it.

"Of all human pursuits, the pursuit of wisdom is the most perfect, the most sublime, the most useful, and the most agreeable."
Thomas Aquinas (1225-1274), Philosopher and Theologian

In his book *Powershift: Knowledge, Wealth, and Violence at the Edge of the 21st Century,* Alvin Toffler wrote about the historic trade-off between the powers of wealth and violence — and the emergence of knowledge as a higher quality power. Wealth can be used to acquire armies and weapons to inflict violence — and violence can be used to acquire more wealth. Both force and wealth are primarily win-lose powers where one is traded off for the other. Wealth can multiply with capitalism within limitations though, because of the multiplier effect of capitalism. Knowledge is a superior dynamic that not only has the capability to upset and overcome the balance between wealth and violence — knowledge can also expand without limitations.

> "You are braver than you believe, stronger than you seem, and smarter than you think."
> *Winnie the Pooh*, by A.A. Milne (1882-1956), Author

Knowledge only has value if the possessor has the wisdom to apply it effectively. Wisdom comes from a combination of intelligence — the ability to understand and problem solve — along with the added element of judgement. Wisdom also helps distinguish between IQ (Intelligence Quotient) and EQ (Emotional Quotient). EQ has been demonstrated to be a better indicator of personal success than IQ alone.

> **Emotional Quotient** is the capability of individuals to recognize their own emotions and those of others, discern between different feelings and label them appropriately, use emotional information to guide thinking and behavior, and manage and/or adjust emotions to adapt to environments or achieve one's goal(s).
> *A Dictionary of Psychology*, Oxford University Press

THE FORMULA (OO + RRR + AA) is an effective tool for deciding how to apply knowledge effectively. You can use your brain to store data and to build your knowledge.

I. THE CENTER OF THE UNIVERSE

You can also use your mind's intelligence to apply that knowledge. But if you really want to **Master the Universe** you need to keep learning from each time you apply **THE FORMULA** and adjust according to what you have learned each time you do so in the future.

> "I think it's very important to have a feedback loop, where you're constantly thinking about what you've done and how you could be doing it better. I think that's the single best piece of advice: Constantly think about how you could be doing things better and questioning yourself."
> Elon Musk, (1971-), Founder and CEO of Tesla and SpaceX

The Wisdom Way provides a model for applying THE FORMULA to an interactive process towards achieving wisdom and mastery of the Universe.

**If you want to Master the Universe —
follow The Wisdom Way**

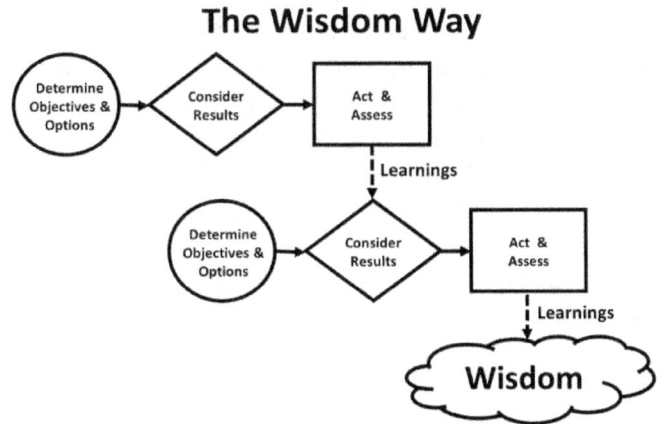

The Wisdom Way is an example of a virtuous cycle, where positive actions contribute to a loop that yields even more positive benefits each time you cycle through the process.

Mastering the Universe is a journey and not a destination. Destinations are endpoints — and endpoints have no future.

Habits and Repetition

The next aspect of Mastering the Universe is the iterative process of habits and repetition. Repeating the effective use of **THE FORMULA (OO + RRR + AA)** will produce a process of continuous improvement.

> "True life is lived when tiny changes occur "
> Leo Tolstoy (1828-1910), Russian Novelist

> "A tiny change today brings a dramatically different tomorrow.:
> Richard Bach (1936-), American Novelist

You can make the most significant impacts on in your life though small, or micro-habits, repeated consistently over time. Success in life typically comes from habits rather than from instant transformations. There are good habits and bad habits — both operate with similar rules, but with vastly different consequences. Positive habits contribute to a virtuous cycle towards success and negative habits contribute to vicious cycles which can lead to failure.

> "Champions keep playing until they get it right."
> Billie Jean King (1943-), Tennis Player

One of the benefits of establishing good habits is that you can accomplish objectives without repeatedly distracting your mind in future, similar situations. There is a risk that you might miss small mistakes sneaking into your routines — so it is a good practice to periodically check the progress and integrity of your habits.

I. THE CENTER OF THE UNIVERSE

Good habits accumulate value over time and are easier to implement when you grow them through small, easy increments. Examples of good habits include stretching every morning in bed before you get up; practicing Deep Breathing every night before you go to sleep; or saving 5% of your earnings every month. You will not get very fit by exercising occasionally, but you will by making a habit of exercising. You will not get much thinner or healthier by dieting one day, but you will by making a habit of following a good diet.

> "If you want to lose weight, *Chase the habit, not the result.*"
> Siobhan (Shiv) Wilson (1991-), British
> Footballer and Trainer

Bad habits can accumulate negative consequences over time. Examples of bad habits include smoking a cigarette after a meal; unhealthy snacking between meals; sitting without activity for too long; or spending all your earnings every month. You can train your body, brain, and mind though micro-habits to program yourself away from bad habits.

> Time is your friend with good habits — and your enemy with bad habits.

It is easier to establish habits if you focus on who you want to be — your desired identity, rather than creating habits based on specific goals. For example, if you decide to identify with being fit, it will be easier to develop exercise and eating habits that relate to being fit. Doing a workout will not make you fit but developing a habit of working out will make you fit. Telling the truth once will not make you an honest person, but a habit of telling the truth will help you develop into an honest person. Using Engaged Thinking once will not make you smarter, but creating a habit of exercising Engaged Thinking and applying **THE FORMULA** will make you more intelligent.

Our self-perceived identities help drive our habits and conversely, our habits drive our self-identity. An identity is something that you can continuously build upon over time as opposed to goals that have finite lifespans. Your body creates a greater increase in dopamine in anticipation of a reward than after the reward. Also, the reward is an endpoint. Instead, you can try to turn it into a virtuous cycle towards your desired identity.

> "Man often becomes what he believes himself to be. If I keep on saying to myself that I cannot do a certain thing, it is possible that I may end by really becoming incapable of doing it. On the contrary, if I have the belief that I can do it, I shall surely acquire the capacity to do it even if I may not have it at the beginning."
> Mahatma Gandhi (1869-1948), Indian Civil Rights Leader

Think about the long-term benefits and don't be too preoccupied with your short-term results. Short term results amount to momentary or minor changes whereas establishing long term habits can create life-changing benefits. Once you establish an easy habit, it is easier to stack on other related habits. Create small wins, and then add new habits.

> "The most common reaction of the human mind to achievement is not satisfaction, but craving for more."
> *Homo Deus*, by Yuval Noah Harari

Repetition eases the integration of habits or techniques into your everyday life. It creates familiarity, which puts your mind is put in a state of cognitive ease. Repeating something makes it more memorable and more persuasive — it also molds patterns into your behavior. It creates habits — good habits or bad habits. Make it your choice. You can decide which habits you want to strengthen.

I. THE CENTER OF THE UNIVERSE

> "Satisfaction lies in the effort, not in the attainment."
> Mahatma Gandhi (1869-1948), Indian Civil Rights Leader

The natural familiarity by way of repetition helps break through the natural defense systems that might resist change. When a behavior has been effective for the survival of an entity, the entity can be resistant to changes that might disrupt the status quo. This resistance to change is natural. If there is no resistance to a change, you might question whether you have made any significant changes.

> "10,000-Hour Rule — the key to achieving world-class expertise in any skill, is, to a large extent, a matter of practicing the correct way, for a total of around 10,000 hours."
> Malcolm Gladwell (1963-), Author and Public Speaker

The number of times you execute a habit is more important than the timespan. You do not have to literally apply 10,000 hours of practice to **THE FORMULA (OO + RRR + AA)** to reap the rewards of your efforts. In fact, the number of hours required to achieve mastery and the relative importance of other factors has been widely debated. Every time you successfully implement **THE FORMULA** enables you to more effectively **Master the Universe**.

You can link physical triggers to specific behaviors to help condition those behaviors. For example, if you make a habit of pressing your thumb to your index finger when you practice Deep-Breathing, you can use this trigger in a pressure situation to condition yourself to invoke the Deep-Breathing process to relax. You can pick different triggers for other situations, such as associating another action with pausing to employ **THE FORMULA**.

Try to reduce friction towards practicing desired habits and add friction to situations that could facilitate bad habits.

Spend time with people or groups with similar identity aspirations and avoid spending time with people who have undesirable habits.

Habits can also be deprogrammed by associating negative behavioral triggers to a habit. One study reportedly found that a highly effective technique was to place two identical, clean ashtrays on a person's desk or workplace at the beginning each day. Then letting the same one fill up all day with the butts and ashes from every cigarette smoked during the day and leaving the other one clean. In less than two months, a significant number of subjects simply stopped smoking. Looking at the clean and pristine ashtray every day overpowered their association of smoking with the dirty ashtray.

People who want to improve their self-esteem can create a habit of self-affirmation practices to develop a more confident self-identity. An example of this is to review a list of what they like about themselves every night before they go to sleep. Thinking about what went well that day helps calm their minds and improve their sleep cycle. They can go through the same process every morning to embolden their day.

The more you practice habits like personal improvement techniques for mindful breathing or behavioral modification, the more proficient you will become. The more frequently you practice effective public speaking techniques, the more comfortable and successful you will be at public speaking. And the more you practice **THE FORMULA (OO + RRR + AA)**, the more it will become a natural habit. You will not become much wiser by applying **THE FORMULA** one time, but you will by making a habit of it and applying your learnings into the cycle of **The Wisdom Way**.

Identify your strengths and desired strengths — then exercise them repetitively and build them like muscles.

I. THE CENTER OF THE UNIVERSE

"Continuous effort — not strength or intelligence — is the key to unlocking our potential."
Sir Winston Churchill (1874 – 1965), British Prime Minister

Memory Skills

Repetition is a powerful tool towards improving your memory too.

How to remember anything that you really want to remember:

1. **Quiz yourself** – forces you to repeat it, which makes it stickier and easier to remember. The fact that you may have forgotten some of the information will help it stand out for future recall.
2. **Summarize and share it with someone else** – you will have a memory of discussing it.
3. **Connect** – what you just learned to experiences you previously had.

Adam Grant (1981-), Wharton professor

Your mind absorbs more information than you can easily recall. One of the challenges is to keep the information fresh and assessable. It helps to apply the spaced repetition process to optimize your memory retention.

An effective spaced repetition technique is to study a subject before you go to sleep and then do a quick review in the morning. Memory processing during sleep helps form and solidify memories. A 2016 study published in Psychology Science determined that bookmarking your study with a sleep cycle reduced effort to memorize information while improving long term retention by 50 percent.

There are also association techniques that can help your recall process. Memory experts sometimes create vivid stories where they substitute a list of items they want to recall to the storyline. For example, they may have a visual storyline where [A] walks up to a house and sees a [B} in a tree. When they ring the doorbell a [C] falls off the roof and the door opens, a [D] appears at the door holding a [E], and so on. The more absurd the story, the easier it is to recall the objects and their sequence. Note: visual associations work better for people who have strong visual modalities as I will discuss in the section on NLP. There are a wide range of memory enhancement techniques such as this that you can research, practice and perfect.

"I don't mind learning something new every day, but then they expect you to remember it too."
Dennis the Menace, Cartoon by Hank Ketcham (1920-2001)

Another of the techniques that memory experts use to improve their recall is to associate outlandish visual images to items they want to recall. For instance, when you meet a person named Bill, you could conjure up the image of the person handing you a bill or associating the person with a duck bill on their face. This technique might work more effectively for someone with a visual recall bias. If you have an auditory recall bias, you might want to associate a song, like Billy Jean to a person named Bill. I will explore recall biases more extensively in the section on NLP & NAC.

Space and Timing

Leveraging space is another tool to help **Master the Universe**. Space is an aspect of a Universe that supports the natural positioning of entities within a Universe — and the natural positioning between different Universes.

I. THE CENTER OF THE UNIVERSE

"Look at this page. What fills up most of this page? Space!

There's space around the borders of the page, space between the lines, space between the words, and space between the characters.

For example, try to read the following line without space between the words in these sentences.

Howeasyisittoreadthissentancewithoutanyspace betweenthewords?Furthermorehowdifficulwouldit betoreadthiswholdpageiftherewasnospacebetweent helinesorbordersofthepage?"

Alan Carroll, Communications skills expert and author

Space has reciprocal characteristics to the properties of glue. Whereas glue holds objects together, space holds objects and entities apart in their natural positions with respect to each other. I will discuss how the effective use of space can improve your ability to center yourself, communicate with others, and improve relationships.

Read the following phrase out loud — "opportunityisnowhere."

Spacing makes the difference between "opportunity is now here" and "opportunity is nowhere" — which makes all the difference in the world.

Space can be an aspect of distance between physical objects, or it can be space in the timing of your actions or speech. The effective use of a pause is a method for inserting space into verbal communications. You can significantly improve your one-to-one communication skills by pausing throughout a conversation. This adds to your perceived credibility, it gives the other party time to absorb your statements and gives you time to listen to their responses.

The effective use of the Power of the Pause can have a dramatic effect on your public speaking skills too. Most importantly, pausing gives you time to take a breath and use your Engaged Thinking process to determine your objectives and consider the potential reactions to your statements.

> "The notes, I handle no better than many pianists. But the pauses between the notes — ah, that is where the art resides."
> Artur Schnabel (1882–1951) Pianist and composer

The adages about waiting for a count of ten before reacting when you are angry or sleeping on a topic before reacting are examples of employing the Power of the Pause. These practices give you the time to think through **THE FORMULA (OO + RRR + AA)** before reacting.

> "The right word may be effective, but no word was ever as effective as a rightly timed pause."
> Mark Twain (1835–1910) American author

Balance

Improving your balance and synchronicity are additional factors towards Mastering the Universe. These factors impact the operational effectiveness of your own soul/mind-brain/body interactions. Individual components of your body are more efficient if they are balanced and synchronized from the perspectives of timing and intensity. They also impact your effectiveness in mastering your interactions with other Universes.

Performing the same exact actions with different timing or intensities can become the difference between success and failure. There are many personal and interpersonal examples of this phenomena including physical conditioning programs, chess games, sports matches, or other interpersonal interactions. You can take the same exact actions with wildly varying results depending on your balance, timing, and sequencing.

Your mind can be utilized to program your brain towards

I. THE CENTER OF THE UNIVERSE

behaviors and timing that create a more effective balance between the different components of your body. There is a bilateral relationship between the actions of your mind and your body. Mental activities and emotions can impact your body just as actions of your body can impact your emotional and mental attitude. Improved mindfulness will enable you to master your body more effectively, just as a well-managed body will enable you to improve your mental abilities.

You can employ **THE FORMULA (OO + RRR + AA)** towards effective balance and synchronicity. **Determine Objectives** – What do you want to achieve? **Consider Reactions** – Based on the different timing and intensities, what actions do you think will accomplish the optimal results. **Action** – follow through, learn from the results; **Assess** and modify your timing and sequencing appropriately the next time you are in a similar situation.

A healthy balance between activities of your mind and body can help extend your physical life as well as increase the enjoyment of your time in the physical world. Likewise, the balance and timing of your behaviors with others will impact your success at impacting other people's behaviors. I will discuss these concepts more thoroughly and provide some specific examples in other sections of the book.

**If you want to Master the Universe —
follow The Wisdom Way**

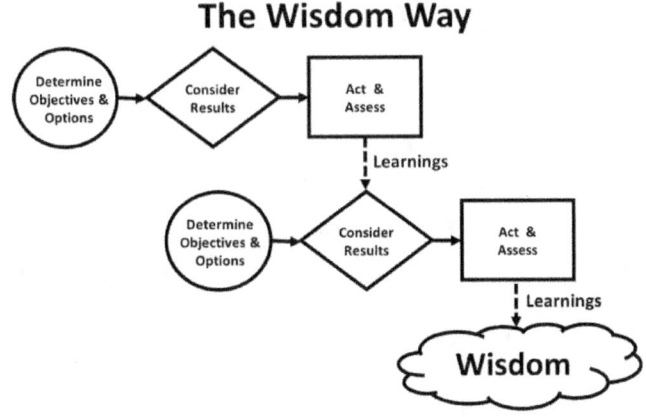

How To MASTER THE UNIVERSE
Personal and Professional Life-Skills Guide

Mastering the Universe is a journey and not a destination. Destinations are endpoints — and endpoints have no future.

Embrace the destinations — and then move on to enjoy the journey.

II. MASTERING YOUR UNIVERSE

You are the **Center of the Universe** — the Center of your Universe.

From your perspective, everything revolves around you. The objective of this section is to discuss methods of applying THE FORMULA to master your personal life.

Master The Universe Formula
THE FORMULA = OO + RRR + AA

1. **OO** – Determine your Objectives and Options.
2. **RRR** – Consider potential Results, Reactions, and Rewards to determine your course of action.
3. **AA** – Act and Assess.

PRO TIP: Use the condensed acronym **"ORA"** to remember **THE FORMULA.**

The intended Reaction to this section is to create a more satisfying life for yourself, which in turn, will make it easier to master other Universes. The strategies and techniques in this section will provide options for you to Act upon to achieve this objective. Several of the concepts in this section will be applicable and expanded towards mastering your interpersonal and professional lives in subsequent sections of the book.

Many people struggle with self-awareness, let alone other-awareness — which is the awareness of other entities and their Universes.

Self-Awareness: Conscious knowledge of one's own character and feelings.
Oxford Dictionary

Self-Awareness also includes an awareness of your current abilities as well as your limitations. This is important towards deciding on which abilities you want to expand and the limitations that you want to minimize.

Think about the Universe of a new child. Immediately after birth, the child is only aware of itself and its basic personal needs — breathing, drinking, eating, sleeping, and the other bodily functions. When a child is born, there is a new Center of the Universe, so be forewarned! If you are a first-time parent, your lifestyle is in for a radical change.

> One of my siblings was born when I was fourteen. So, at a relatively early age, I was able to observe firsthand the **COTU Principle** applied to a newborn. Most children are totally self-centered at birth and are treated as if they are the center of the universe.
>
> When someone tells me that they have are expecting a new child, I jokingly tell them that there will be a new "center of the universe."

Once someone is born, they start experiencing life in this world while slowly becoming aware of other entities and the impacts of cause and effect from their actions. They become aware that there are other people, creatures, and entities in the world — our parents or caregivers, pets, sounds, and other objects. Some people remain self-centered, and others mature out of this behavioral pattern. The quality of our interactions with other entities can help satisfy some of our basic personal needs and expand into satisfying higher level needs.

Let's explore how we can get the best results from ourselves before exploring techniques to master our interpersonal relationships. I will discuss techniques for mastering your core being — or centering yourself. Relating back to the discussion on operating systems, think of your spirit as being like a control tower for a vehicle — your body. You can abstract your mind from your body and direct how you want your body and behaviors to perform. This can be challenging because you already have pre-programmed behaviors etched into your system from genetics and past experiences. The key is to take responsibility for your decisions, consider your options, the consequences, act, and then assess the results. If you want to perfect and program repetitive behaviors — you need to practice. Even then, there may be limitations on how much your body is capable of changing. Fortunately, you have a considerable ability to stretch the envelope.

Maslow's Pyramid

Reviewing Maslow's Hierarchy of Needs will provide a perspective on what drives our fundamental behaviors. **Maslow's Hierarchy of Needs,** also nicknamed **Maslow's Pyramid,** is a psychology theory developed by Abraham Maslow in 1943, that uses a pyramid to illustrate five different levels of human needs.

The most basic level is Physiological Needs addresses the basic personal needs such as breathing, drinking, eating, and sleeping — which are requirements for physiological survival. If you are unable to satisfy the physiological level your operating system, you could even end up without a body to experience the physical world. In other words — you can die.

The next level entails Safety Needs, then Social Needs, followed by Self-Esteem Needs. The final and highest level, Self-Actualization, refers to the pinnacle of achieving one's full potential which includes altruism and spirituality. The theory is that people's behaviors are generally motivated to satisfy the lower levels of needs before they can effectively progress to satisfying the next levels of these needs. For example, if someone or their family is starving, they are motivated to risk compromising higher level principles such as Safety, Esteem and Self-Actualization by stealing food. It is worth noting that the pyramid is just a two-dimensional representation of a hierarchy of needs and, the lines between the levels of needs are not hard lines. There are often overlaps between the migration up the levels of the pyramid of needs, and Maslow leaves some flexibility in his theory based on individual situations.

Mastering your Universe can be applied to satisfying all of your needs in the pyramid. Keep in mind that everyone else you interact with is operating under their own hierarchy of needs under the **COTU Principle**.

> **COTU Principle:** Every entity is the Center of its own Universe and is motivated by its own survival and success.

The bottom of Maslow's Pyramid focuses on the Survival, and the Thriving builds as you ascend the levels of the pyramid. The lower levels of the pyramid are more strongly related to satisfying the needs of your body and the higher levels are more relevant to the needs of your Soul.

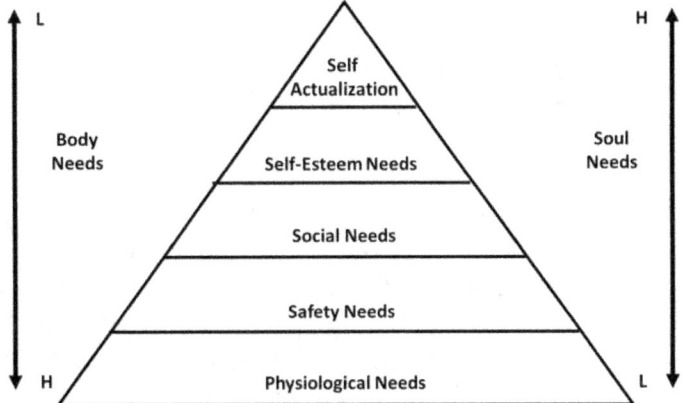

Mindfulness

"I don't live in either my past or my future. I'm interested only in the present. If you can concentrate always on the present, you'll be a happy man. Life will be a party for you, a grand festival, because life is the moment we're living now"
The Alchemist by Paulo Coelho

Mindfulness is an awareness of what is happening now. It is a mental state achieved by a relaxed focus on the present moment — experiencing thoughts, feelings, and sensations without judgment. Mindfulness can help you relax and increases your appreciation of life by minimizing stress and reducing your attention to pain. It involves the variation of the thinking processes that I am referring to as Mindful Thinking.

Mindful Thinking can be achieved by detaching yourself from your Reflexive and Engaged Thinking processes. This detachment allows you to rest and refresh from the pressures of the other two thinking modes. It also helps you connect to the Extended Mind, which I touch on in the section on Cosmic Balance.

> "Quiet the mind, and the soul will speak."
> Buddha (463-483 BC or 480-400BC),
> Religious Leader

When you practice mindfulness, you abstract your mind from external and internal distractions while appreciating the moment. It helps synchronize your soul/mind with your brain/body. If your mind is jumping around, uncontrolled from thought-to-thought, you will have difficulty achieving effective results. One of the goals of Mindfulness is reaching a state of non-Thought where you free up your mind to connect and synchronize with the Cosmos. Removing distractions helps unlock the full potential of your mind.

> "Until you make the unconscious conscious, it will direct your life and you will call it fate."
> Carl Jung (1875-1961), Psychiatrist

One of my strategies for studying for exams at Tulane University was to make sure that my mind was fresh for a test.

I had friends who would study all night before a test to cram as much information in their brains as possible. Consequently, their brains would be exhausted by test time, and they would have trouble thinking clearly and recalling information during the test.

For my first mid-term, I decided to do some yoga and meditate before going to sleep early. I managed to achieve what felt like an enhanced state of semi-consciousness.

When I woke up, I felt like my mind could pull information out of the air and instantly access any knowledge I had previously acquired. I aced the test and more importantly, it was an exhilarating experience — that gradually wore off during the day.

II. MASTERING YOUR UNIVERSE

There are many practices and activities that can help you achieve better results with Mindfulness. If you focus deeply on an immediate sight, sound, smell, or tactile sensation, you can take a break from thinking about the past or future — while reducing stress and anxiety. You can utilize some of your favorite activities discussed in this section, such as exercise, yoga, meditation — even eating, drinking, breathing, or listening to music to help you center yourself more effectively.

> **Yoga:** union of the self with the Supreme Being or ultimate principle.
> *Dictionary.com*

Your Reflexive Thinking may try to interfere with achieving mindfulness because it can create constant interruptions. We can only concentrate on a few tasks at a time, so you need to reduce disruptions. The highly diverse operations of Reflexive Thinking have one feature in common — they require attention and are disrupted when attention is drawn away. Mindful Thinking comes from a conscious decision and distinguishes it from pure Reflexive Thinking — which is triggered by reactive stimuli.

> Our minds are like the captain of a ship, steering our bodies and lives though the sea. If your mind is constantly interrupted by thoughts of the past or the future, it becomes like the captain of a ship constantly grabbing the wheel, steering the ship in different directions, and zigzagging erratically through the ocean of life.

Mindful Thinking can help you avoid distracting thoughts that take your focus away from achieving your objectives.

> "Don't think about the future. Just be here now. Don't think about the past. Just be here now."
> Ram Dass (1931-2019), Author and Harvard professor

"Don't worry, be happy."
Bobbie McFerrin, (1950-), Musician

While mindfulness helps you focus on appreciating your present state, it is also worthwhile to set aside separate time slots to think about the past and future. You can consider what you want to accomplish in the future as with the first step of **THE FORMULA (OO + RRR + AA).** You can also learn from the past and assess the results of previous actions as with the last step of **THE FORMULA.** Thinking about the future and past are complementary to focusing on the moment. Just separate and allocate this time consciously while prioritizing space to appreciate the current moment of time.

"I live in the present. I only remember the past and anticipate the future."
Henry David Thoreau (1817-1862), Author

"Confine yourself to the present."
"Never let the future disturb you. You will meet it, if you have to, with the same weapons of reason which today arm you against the present."
Marcus Aurelius (121-180 AD), Roman Emperor

Whether you are thinking about past, present, or future moments, you will be more successful if you can keep your mind focused on a single train of thought at a time. Fundamental techniques for achieving mindfulness begin with focusing on the functional needs of a new child – breathing, eating, and other basic survival needs.

"Yesterday is history. Tomorrow is a mystery. Today is a gift. That's why we call it 'The Present.'"
Eleanor Roosevelt (1884-1962), First Lady of the United States

II. MASTERING YOUR UNIVERSE

"Yesterday is gone. Tomorrow has not yet come. We have only today. Let us begin."
Mother Teresa (1910-1997), Saint, Missionary and Nun

Your Body

You have a short lease on the use of your body to interact in the physical world. If you take good care of your body to improve its operation, it will be easier for your mind to connect and master your interactions with the rest of the physical world. You have an opportunity to get more enjoyment and satisfaction out of your physical life by mastering your body first — then you can be more effective at mastering your behaviors.

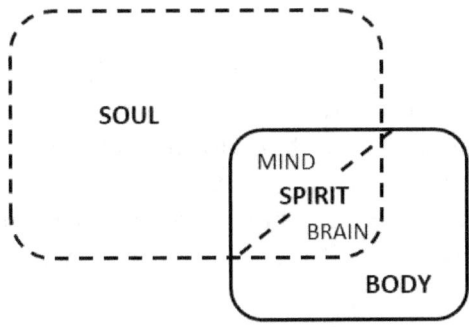

Using your mind to master your body can even help you expand your physiological limits towards mastering the effects of the physical environment.

In high school, I was on a springboard diving team in Florida during the winter months. Even though it was in Florida, the temperatures sometimes got down to the low 40 degrees Fahrenheit.

One evening we even had a diving competition in an unheated pool. We had capes to warm us between dives, but we had to stand on the board wearing nothing but a small nylon swimsuit during our diving routines. When you are standing on the board, preparing for your dive, you need to calm your body and focus your concentration on the dive you are about to perform — which can be difficult when you are shaking and shivering from the cold weather.

I decided to try to apply breathing and mind-over-body control techniques that I learned from my yoga practices to master my reactions to the moderately cold temperatures. I surmised that if I could master my physiology to behave as if it was warm, I would feel warmer. I would slow my breath to the rate as if I felt warm, relax my body to stop shaking and hold my shoulders back as if I were warm. I would think about keeping the cold on the outside of my body. Applying these techniques helped me feel warm enough to concentrate on my dive.

You can also use your mind and the upcoming behavioral conditioning techniques to overcome some levels of hunger and pain. For example, if you chose to diet to achieve a healthy weight, you are typically choosing to accept a certain level of hunger. If you embrace hunger as an interesting feeling instead of considering it a feeling of pain, you can accept moderate levels of hunger.

When three-time Ironman Triathlon World Champion Craig Alexander Master was asked how he overcomes the pain at the break point of an event, he said that he separates pain into two categories — sweet pain and sour pain.

When Craig decides to compete in a triathlon, sweet pain is part of the package. He accepts it because he made the choice.

II. MASTERING YOUR UNIVERSE

Breathing Skills

Learning how to breathe effectively addresses the most basic physiological needs first — as reflected in Maslow's Pyramid. If you stop breathing — you die. You die faster than you would from the loss of any of your other physiological survival needs. On the positive side, mastering your breathing skills provides a gateway for mastering mindfulness and other skills covered in this book.

> You have a finite number of breaths, so make them count.

We all breathe, but most people fail to practice effective breathing techniques. Proper breathing gives us time and space to satisfy our other basic needs, and then to expand up Maslow's Pyramid, and on to master the rest of your Universe. Proper breathing techniques can help us to center ourselves and be more effective at interacting with others. An example that I will address later is the use of breathing exercises to center and calm ourselves for more effective public speaking.

> The number one rule in scuba diving is to **never stop breathing**. This might sound simplistic on the surface, but it is very literal, life-critical advice for scuba diving. The deeper you dive; the more external water pressure is exerted on your body and lungs.
> As you ascend, the external pressure lessens and the air in your lungs expands. If you hold your breath while ascending, you run the risk of the air pressure in your lungs expanding to the point of bursting your lungs.
> Continually breathing enables the air pressure in your lungs to adjust to the change in external pressure on your body.

Have you ever experienced shortness of breath and a

rapid heart rate before an important event? Before a meeting or speaking in public? Or before a sports activity? Employing an effective breathing practice can help you relax and focus on the task at hand. There are several variations of breathing exercises that primarily center around breathing more slowly and deeper than normal, while only focusing on your breath.

> "No matter what you eat, how much you exercise, how resilient your genes are, how skinny or young or wise you are, none of it matters if you're not breathing properly. There is nothing more essential to our health and wellbeing than breathing: take air in, let it out, repeat 25,000 times a day. Yet, as a species, humans have lost the ability to breathe correctly, with grave consequences."
> James Nestor, Science Journalist

There are three steps to a basic breathing practice — slowly breathing in through your nose to completely fill your lungs; holding your breath; and then slowly breathing out to completely empty your lungs.

Breathing through your nose is important to compress and process the oxygen effectively. According to Nobel laureate Louis Ignarro, nasal tissues produce a gas known as Nitric Oxide (NO or Nitric Monoxide), which enhances lung functions and increases oxygen levels by 20 percent. It also has antiviral properties that help defend against infection. Researchers have shown that mouth breathing can decimate Nitric Oxide, conversely, nasal breathing increases Nitric Oxide.

Breathing in slowly and holding your breath helps maximize your oxygen availability — and breathing out slowly optimizes your body's Carbon Dioxide exposure. Carbon Dioxide also triggers cells to absorb the oxygen and decreases inflammation in our bodies.

Studies at Stanford University have demonstrated that most people take an average of twenty breaths per minute —

with an oxygen absorption efficiency rate of only 50 percent. When you breathe properly at the rate of six breaths per minute you can increase your absorption rate to 85 percent – an amazing 70% improvement in efficiency. Imagine the positive effect this can have on your performance and wellbeing.

4-2-4 Basic Breathing Technique:

1. **Slowly breathe in through your nose for about four (4) seconds**, filling in the bottom of your lungs into your stomach first, expanding to the middle of your lungs and finally the top of your lungs until you have completely filled and expanded your lungs with fresh oxygen.
2. **Hold your breath for about two (2) seconds**, letting your lungs absorb the oxygen.
3. **Slowly exhale for about four (4) seconds** while reversing the process. Exhaling from the top or your lungs, then the middle, and finally the bottom of your lungs until you have emptied your lungs of nitric oxide and carbon dioxide.

Pro Tips:
- After breathing out completely, immediately return to breathing in, and repeat the process. Do not leave your lungs devoid of oxygen, nitric oxide, and carbon dioxide.
- One second is a recommended time period for a count, but you can build up to that level.
- The act of holding your breath between inhales and exhales increases your exposure to nitric oxide and carbon dioxide to assist oxygen absorption.
- Expand your diaphragm downward to start your inhalation and contract it upwards to finish your exhalation.

- Counting helps you focus on breathing instead of other distractions. It also helps regulate your oxygen intake. You can substitute mantras, other mindfulness techniques or simply breathing as the process becomes more natural to your body. Once you are proficient at the process, you may decide to practice deep breathing without needing to count.

A second technique is to find a comfortable seated position on a chair or stool, with your feet on the floor, your thighs parallel to the ground, and your back in a straight posture without touching the back of a chair. You can also perform this technique while seated in a lotus position with a straight spinal posture too. Rest your hands upwards on the juncture of your legs and stomach. Breath slowly and deeply while tensing all of the muscles in your body, and then exhale in two puffs while relaxing your body. Do this at least three times and then breathe slowly for at least three counts, relaxing the whole time and focusing your closed eyes on the point between your eyebrows. This focal point is sometimes called the Third Eye, the Mind's Eye, or the Inner Eye.

A more complex technique is called the 4-7-8 breathing method, which was developed by Dr. Andrew Weil. It is based on pranayama — a traditional yogic breathing technique.

4-7-8 Breathing Technique:

1. Start by positioning your tongue behind your front teeth, resting it against the roof of your mouth and keep it there. Exhale completely through your mouth around your tongue, making a whooshing sound.
2. Inhale and fill your lungs through your nose for four (4) seconds.

3. Hold your breath for seven (7) seconds.
4. Completely release your breath through your mouth making a whooshing sound for eight (8) seconds — starting with the top of your lungs and working your way to the bottom of your lungs.
5. Repeat steps 2-4 for at least three more cycles.

Pro Tips:
- Find a comfortable place to sit and keep your back straight.
- After breathing out completely, immediately return to breathing in, and repeat the process. Do not leave your lungs devoid of oxygen, nitric oxide, and carbon dioxide.
- Expand your diaphragm downward to start your inhalation and contract it upwards to finish your exhalation.

You can also incorporate a self-hypnotism technique into your breathing practice by counting down the number of breaths from 20 to 1 as you practice your breathing technique, keeping all other distracting thoughts out of your mind. Even deep breathing from a count of 10 down to 1 will help if you are short on time. You can also add and repeat a mantra at the end of your breathing practice to help relax and ingrain the mantra into your subconsciousness.

There are other versions of this practice that recommend different breath counts, and it is important to breathe slowly and deeply. In any event, go directly to inhaling after you finish your exhale to inhaling again. Since we are all different, try experimenting to find the different variations of deep breathing techniques to uncover the technique that works best for you. It is also fine to alternate between methods.

Try to repeat your favorite breathing practice for at least four to six breaths at a time to help you relax and focus on higher level activities and objectives. If you can take a moment before responding to a question, or prior to public speaking — even one or two deep breaths will help you relax and center yourself.

There are times when you may feel sick — for example when you are congested and have trouble breathing. These times provide a contrast to help you appreciate the times when you are feeling well. Take the time when you are feeling well to focus on how wonderful it is to take full, slow, breaths of fresh air and enjoy how great it is to feel well. In fact, take time to do this every day to better appreciate life.

Breathing properly through your nose also helps improve your health by reducing inflammation in your lungs. If you are like most people, you have been spending most of your life breathing inefficiently. It takes effort and repetition to change such a deeply ingrained habit. You can practice proper breathing when you wake up, when you go to sleep, and whenever you want to focus on the moment. If you take the time to frequently practice proper breathing skills, you will eventually make it a subconscious habit that helps your body and mind operate more effectively.

"Breathe. Let go. And remind yourself that this very moment is the only one you know you have for sure."
Oprah Winfrey (1954-), Talk Show Host and Author

Fuel

"In Heaven there is no beer; That's why we drink it here."
The Polka Stars

Your body needs food and drinks to survive and thrive. The better the quality of fuel that you provide your body, the better it will perform. Food and drinks also provide an avenue towards increased enjoyment of life — so it is worthwhile to consider your preferred balance between your health and pleasure objectives. **THE FORMULA (OO + RRR + AA)** applies to your choice of quality and quantity of fuel consumption. Determine your objectives and options, consider the reactions, assess the results of your actions, and adjust accordingly the next time.

Deep Breathing before eating stimulates your parasympathetic nervous system, which is one of three autonomic systems that stimulate Reflexive responses. The parasympathetic nervous system is responsible for stimulating "rest and digest" responses, whereas the sympathetic nervous system is responsible for stimulating "flight or fight" responses — and the enteric nervous system controls autonomic motor functions.

You can apply mindfulness techniques to maximize the quality of digestion and the pleasure of consumption. If you slow down and take a moment to focus on the qualities of shape, colors, presentation, smell, taste, and texture of the food and drink – you will have a greater appreciation of what you are about to consume. Try to appreciate whatever you are drinking at the time — whether it is water, wine, juice, milk, or another favorite of yours.

> Wine and culinary enthusiasts claim that there are different taste regions on your tongue for sweet in the front, salty & sour on the sides, bitter in the back — and now umami as the fifth taste. Scientific studies have concluded that taste receptors are found all over the tongue, though some areas are slightly more sensitive to certain tastes than others.

Likewise, try to take a moment to enjoy the food you are eating. Take a brief break from all the other distracting thoughts, and savor the tastes, smell, textures, and visuals of the food you are experiencing.

I have often noticed people who are too busy talking or thinking about their next comment to take a deep breath and enjoy their food or drinks. Try to take a mindful break to appreciate your food and drinks. You will also create time to listen and learn from the other people around you.

"A party without a cake is really just a meeting."
Julia Child (1912-2004), Cooking Author

Sleep

Achieving quality sleep sessions is an extremely important part of satisfying your basic physiological needs and improving the effectiveness of your operating system. Sleeping is important. You spend approximately one third of your life sleeping. Sleeping rests your body and provides a break from the intensive activities between your mind and brain. Recent studies have identified another important function that the sleep cycle performs for the brain — cleaning or clearing your brain.

Whereas the brain only occupies around two percent of the body mass — it uses up twenty-five percent of the nutrients.

The brain does not have a separate lymphatic system to drain waste like the rest of your body — so the brain uses your body's sleeping cycle to clear out the toxins. During the sleep cycle, the brain cells get a chance to rest. Studies utilizing MRI machines during sleep cycles have demonstrated that large, slow waves of cerebrospinal fluids wash over the brain, causing the neurons to synchronize by turning on and off at the same time. When they stop at the same time, they do not need as much oxygen. The reduction of blood flow enables space for the cerebrospinal fluid to flow in and wash away toxins that have built up during the day. So, a good night's sleep really does have a cleansing effect on your brain.

> "Sleeping — A carwash for you brain."
> Jessica Stillman, Inc.com, Nov 10, 2019

There are many techniques that can help you achieve a better night's sleep. Mindful breathing can help when you go to bed, or if you wake up in the middle of the night. You can try repeating the breathing countdown practice to help clear the mind, adding a mantra, or other meditative practices. As mentioned in the Breathing section, slow breathing stimulates "rest and digest" responses in your parasympathetic nervous system. It also helps to avoid heavy food, alcohol and blue light from TV, computers, or mobile phones for an hour or two before trying to sleep.

The physical, relaxed state of sleep frees up your mind's imagination to explore ideas. Your mind can act like a movie scriptwriter trying out different plots, sub-plots, and scenes — and then revising them over time.

> Some of my best ideas come to me between three to seven in the morning. It is a time when my soul seems to have easier access — through my mind — to my brain.

The relaxed, semi-conscious sleep state between being awake and asleep is known as the hypnagogic state. This state can open a gateway for your sub-conscious mind to problem solve and explore creative ideas. Embrace the opportunity. Creative geniuses such as Salvadore Dali, Isaac Newton, Beethoven, and Thomas Edison used to take advantage of this state of mind to stimulate their thought process. If your mind is too busy as you are falling asleep, you might want to get up, capture the thoughts on paper, smartphone, or computer to clear your mind and bookmark the ideas for when you wake up — and then go back to bed for some more sleep or contemplation.

Salvadore Dali used to go to sleep with a canvas next to his bed. Many of his famous works were inspired by what he saw in his mind when he started to go to sleep or when he initially woke up from sleep. Dali would sometimes sit in a chair as he was falling asleep, hold a spoon between his thumb and finger and place a plate directly beneath the spoon.

As he was falling asleep, the spoon would fall onto the plate, it would wake him up in a hallucinatory-like, semiconscious state — and he would capture his creative visions on the canvas. Thomas Edison used a similar technique with steel balls.

Mantras

A mantra or a chant is the practice of repeating a sound, word, or phrase to help you focus your thoughts and achieve mindfulness. The mantra or chant is often repeated melodically — the repetition can have a hypnotic effect or help imprint a message into your brain. The use of mantras can be traced through religions and cultures around the world including African, Pacific Island, European, Asian, Native American, and Aboriginal Australian cultures. Some practices believe that a chant or mantra helps with your spiritual development, which would reinforce the concept of using a chant to help your brain/body connect with your mind/soul via your spirit. A common one-word mantra used in yoga is a repeated chanting of the word "Om" — as if slowly spelling out the letters A-U-M.

One of my favorite mantras is adapted from a book called *Living Buddha, Living Christ*, where Thich Nhat Hanh writes about the similarities between Buddhism and Christianity. The four lines of the mantra are:

II. MASTERING YOUR UNIVERSE

Calming
Smiling
Present Moment
Beautiful Moment

I incorporate the mantra into my breathing practice. I say or think "Calming" while slowly breathing in and hesitating, followed by saying or thinking "Smiling" while slowly exhaling. Then I say or think "Present Moment" while slowly breathing in and hesitating; followed by "Beautiful Moment" as I am slowly exhaling.

I repeat this mantra multiple times until I have achieved a desired relaxed state of mind and body.

Try a few different mantras and pick one or more that are meaningful to you. Repeating your favorite mantra can lead you into a state of pleasant mindfulness.

Meditation

Meditation is a formal practice to help achieve mindfulness. It provides a methodology to train yourself to achieve a more relaxed focus — which can then be applied to other activities. There are multiple forms of meditation that involve postures such as Hatha Yoga or breathing practices and chants/mantras as discussed above. A common element of most meditation practices is developing the ability to focus on one thing at a time and eventually being able to achieve a state of Non-Thought or Mindful Thinking — which involves the ability to totally clear and refresh your mind from distractions. In Hatha Yoga, you can start with practicing a breathing technique as described above, then practice focusing on one physical position at a time — and the evolution of movement and balance from one position to another. While performing the practice, try to clear all other distractions from your mind.

You can achieve similar results from other forms of

exercise like running or swimming — where you can focus on your stride, your stroke, your breathing, or other elements of the exercise. If you practice chanting in monasteries, mantras in yoga, or other forms of word repetition, you are practicing the ability to focus on one thing at a time — the chant or mantra.

In 2011, Psychiatry Research: Neuroimaging, researchers reported that eight-weeks of engaging in an average of 27 minutes a day of meditation results in differences in the brain. The study included two groups of people who had never meditated before. One continued to not meditate, while the other was put into a mindfulness-based stress reduction program at the University of Massachusetts Center for Mindfulness.

Magnetic Resonance Images (MRIs) were taken of the brain structure of the 16 participants two weeks before and two weeks after they took part in the program, which included meditation that focused on non-judgmental awareness of sensations, feelings, and the state of their mind. These brain scans revealed that the group that meditated, compared to the group that did not, had increased gray-matter density in the brain's hippocampus and decreased gray-matter density in the amygdala.

Interestingly, the amygdala interacts with the body's "fight-or-flight" response while the hippocampus is involved with introspection, learning, and memory.

Amishi Jha, a neuroscientist who was not a part of this study, told The Harvard Gazette that these results shed "light on the mechanism of action of mindfulness-based training," showing that stress can not only be reduced after eight weeks of this training but also that training corresponds to structural changes in the brain.

Other work by the same team has also found that meditation causes 50-year-old meditators to have the same amount of gray matter as typical 25-year-old.

Most of us invest time every morning cleansing and preparing our bodies for the day ahead. We invest time in activities like showering, brushing our teeth, and shaving. Why not prioritize twenty minutes each morning to cleansing and preparing our minds through meditation? This investment will return more than the twenty minutes to your day through the efficiency it will add to your thinking and actions throughout the day. Our minds should be the masters of our bodies.

Exercise

Exercising your body helps increase the effectiveness of your brain, which in turn makes it easier for your mind to manage your activities in the physical world. There are many studies that have proven the positive effects of exercise on your brain's performance and general mood.

> "Exercise is the most transformative thing that you can do for your brain today . . . "
> Wendy Suzuki, TED Women 2017

Countless studies have demonstrated that there are immediate, short-term effects from even performing a single exercise session which include the increase in neurotransmitters such as dopamine. These create an elevation of your mood while improving your mind's shift and focused attention for up to 2 hours. A continued exercise program of three-to-four, thirty plus minute sessions per week can increase the creation of new brain cells that strengthen your brain and help improve long-term memory.

The message is that your operating system will be much more effective if you take the time to exercise your body, and you will have a longer lease on the time you have to use and enjoy your body.

PAR (Post-Aerobic Reboot) Technique:

The PAR Technique is a hybrid of yoga-style centering and self-rejuvenation techniques. The result is a naturally euphoric effect from "rebooting" your brain and body. The practice can be performed after any aerobic exercise such as jogging, swimming, rowing, or cross-country skiing — exercises where your muscles have been stressed by aerobic activity. This enables you to leverage the post workout slowdown of your heartrate, the increased oxygenated blood flow to your brain, and the euphoric effects from the endorphins generated during your workout.

1. **Aerobic Exercise**
   Perform at least 16-20 minutes of exercise at a consistent aerobic heart rate level. Then reduce your heart rate — letting it drop about halfway back to your normal heart rate.
2. **Reboot**
   Lay flat on your back with your eyes closed and let your body relax while your heartbeat slows down. Being in a horizontal position helps free up the blood flow to your brain by neutralizing the gravitational pull you would experience from a standing or sitting position.
   Empty your mind of distractions and relax your brain to allow the space for toxins to wash out from your brain. Imagine the oxygenated blood and endorphins washing through your body and cleansing your brain. This process of relaxing the mind along with the rest of the body provides a cleansing effect, similar to the effect sleeping has on your body.
3. **Recover**
   Relax until your heart rate has returned to its normal rate — and enjoy the feeling longer if you want to.

Practicing this as you are recovering from an exercise session increases your ability to refresh and recharge your body. When you are ready, sit up for a short period of time to let your blood flow stabilize before standing up. Then enjoy the euphoric and rejuvenating effects of the practice.

Pro Tips:
- Tense your body before Step 2 and then go through the progression of a focus on relaxing your feet, then legs, followed by your arms and hands, your torso, and finally your head, jaws, and face. And then focus on your heart rate and breathing while clearing your mind of all other thoughts. If your body is already relaxed from the exercise, progress directly to your focus on your heart rate and breathing. As you are doing this, focus your closed eyes on the point between your eyebrows.
- Freestyle swimming is an exercise that can naturally incorporate Deep Breathing techniques that are described in this book. During this exercise, you typically take deep breaths above water that you slowly exhale while your head is under the water. One of the few limitations towards implementing an ideal Deep Breathing technique is that your inhale is typically through your mouth instead of your nose.
- Defer to professional medical advice for your specific situation.

A thirty-minute workout only takes about 2% of a 24-hour day and it can significantly reduce the amount of time you need for a good night's sleep. If you make exercise a daily habit, you can improve your body's health and increase your enjoyment of life.

"It is health that is real wealth and not pieces of gold and silver."
Mahatma Gandhi (1869-1948), Indian Civil Rights Leader

Behavioral Modification Skills

There are several approaches towards mastering behaviors by applying the second step of **THE FORMULA (OO + RRR + AA)** to establish rewards (or penalties) related to behavioral habits. Repetitive reinforcement of a reaction to a stimulus can be an effective method of modifying future behaviors — or habits.

The most basic level is using your mind to help master your physical reflexes with techniques such as Classical Conditioning. There are also behavioral modification techniques such as Operant Conditioning and Neuro-Linguistic Programming (NLP) that can be used to modify more sophisticated behavioral habits.

Whereas the previous techniques we discussed are primarily applicable to mastering your own Universe — behavioral modification techniques are also applicable to mastering other Universes.

Your natural physiological reflexes, such as jumping when you hear a loud noise can save your life. Reactions to stimuli like the loud noise are programmed into our behaviors though past experiences and some are genetically programed into our bodies through natural selection during the evolution of our species. Unwanted reactions can be deprogramed through techniques like Classical Conditioning.

Classical Conditioning is a technique for modifying physiological behavior patterns by modifying a basic Stimulus-Response (S-R) pattern. It is done by connecting a previously unconnected stimulus with a natural connected stimulus to generate a newly paired response. This involves associative memory which is core to Reflexive Thinking — and is used to condition physiological, autonomic reflexes.

> In 1897 an experiment was performed by Ivan Pavlov, where he paired the ringing of a metronome with the act of bringing food for a dog. Pavlov observed that dogs salivate when you bring them food. When he repeatedly matched the ringing of a metronome with bringing food to the dog, the dog would eventually be conditioned to salivate at the ringing of the metronome — with or without delivering the food.

Classical Conditioning applies to physiological, reflexive reactions — and the effect evaporates when the matched stimulus is eliminated. For example, when you stop repeatedly ringing the metronome during the food delivery in Pavlov's experiment, the dog will eventually stop salivating to the ringing of the metronome. The conditioning effect can be strengthened if you randomly match the two stimuli together. For example, if you only randomly bring food when you ring the metronome, the salivation response to the metronome will continue for a longer period of time after you stop bringing food at the same time as ringing the metronome. The effective use of repetition is essential to the effectiveness of Classical Conditioning.

> "When we repeat an action over and over again in a given context and then get a reward when you do that, you are learning very slowly and incrementally to associate that context with that behavior."
> Wendy Wood, Psychology Professor at the USC

How To MASTER THE UNIVERSE
Personal and Professional Life-Skills Guide

An approach towards deprogramming yourself to unwanted Classical Conditioning reactions is to break the repetitive stimulus-response chain. If you keep hearing loud noises without dangerous consequences, you can deprogram your responses to the noises. Sometimes this will happen naturally when you hear enough non-threatening loud noises, and you can even interject loud noises in your life to break the programming cycle. Deprogramming these behaviors can give you time to over-ride your Reflexive Thinking with higher quality Engaged Thinking.

> "It only takes 10 or 15 times of somebody really paying attention, whether it's a **mindful** eating exercise or a mindful smoking exercise, that the reward value drops to or even below zero,"
>
> "It turns out, this is where mindfulness comes in. If you want to change behavior, you have to update the reward value. And the only way to update a reward value is to bring awareness in and see very, very clearly what you're actually getting from the behavior."
>
> Dr. Jud Brewer (1974-), Psychiatrist, Neuroscientist, and Author

One of the dangers in distracted or high-pressure situations is for people to suffer what skydivers call "brain-lock," where your mind freezes up and the skydivers fail to deploy perfectly working parachutes. This syndrome can happen to any of us in varying degrees. If you are not accustomed to public speaking and are ready to get on stage, your head can start pounding and the stress involved can block your Engaged Thinking process from over-riding your Reflexive Thinking process. In crisis situations like skydiving, this can mean the difference between dying or surviving.

There is a three-stage process that can help you master a crisis situation.

II. MASTERING YOUR UNIVERSE

Mastering Crisis Situations:

1. **Stay calm** – you can use breathing or mindfulness techniques to calm yourself.
2. **Use situational awareness** – take a moment to assess where you are and what are your priorities.
3. **Never give up** – you will never master the situation if you give up — and you are usually capable of much more than you realize. You want to avoid panicking, brain-lock, or surrendering if you want to master the situation.

"Some Ninety-five percent of the people who die in cold water are not actually hypothermic — with a sub-normal body temperature. The cold does not kill them. It is the terror that leads to drowning and heart attacks. People have a grasp reflex followed by uncontrolled breathing known as hyperventilation. If you gasp for air, you are more likely to inhale freezing water — making it difficult to coordinate your swimming movements if it does not drown you first. There is a 1-10-1 system for surviving a fall into cold water. You have one minute to get your breathing under control. After ten minutes your muscles and nerve fibers get so cold that they do not function anymore — so you have ten minutes to propel yourself to safety. Then you have around one hour before you lose consciousness."
The Survivors Club, By Ben Sherwood (1964-)

A more sophisticated behavioral modification technique is called Operant Conditioning, which was pioneered by B. F. Skinner. In Operant Conditioning, behaviors are conditioned by anticipated reactions. Your responses are trained by anticipated actions instead of the other way around in Classical Conditioning where the repeated stimuli precede the conditioned actions.

An early age example occurs if, whenever a baby cries, the parents come to give the baby attention. Initially the baby might have a valid reason for crying like bodily pain or hunger. If the parents usually come to the rescue whenever the baby cries — the baby learns to cry whenever it wants attention, even if nothing is wrong. The response of crying is initiated based on the anticipated after-the-fact behavior of the parents providing the attention.

The basic process in Operant Conditioning involves repeatedly reinforcing behavior that you would like to have continued — and offering no reinforcement for behavior that you do not want continued. If someone reacts counter to how you would like them to react, negative reinforcement is reinforcement too. So, if you want to stop the reinforcement of the behavior, it is better to not react in any manner.

For example, a service rep, who receives a few negative reactions from customers might be conditioned to have a bad attitude towards customers — which can create a vicious cycle of acting more negatively towards customers — who in turn are more negative towards the service rep. I will discuss more about the effect of negative reinforcement when we discuss modifying another party's behavior.

You can condition your own behavior by repeatedly rewarding yourself for behavior patterns that you would like to reinforce. For example, rewarding yourself whenever you spend a defined number of hours on a project. Or how about rewarding yourself every time that you have successfully applied **THE FORMULA (OO + RRR + AA)**?

There are many ways that you can reward your own behavior. You can set up milestones and goals for actions with rewards such as time off, your favorite food, or a rewarding activity. Even seemingly benevolent behaviors are reinforced by rewards to the instigator. The reward could come from a friendly reaction, a public award, a smile, or just the feeling of self-satisfaction for performing the good deed. The power of repetition is instrumental in conditioning your behavior.

In the next Section, I will discuss how to leverage these techniques to modify the behaviors of other parties. In fact, the very process of modifying someone else's behavior involves modifying your own behavior.

II. MASTERING YOUR UNIVERSE

A counselor at a secondary school performed an experiment utilizing **Operant Conditioning** to help improve the behavior of recalcitrant, troublesome students — students who were consistently reported for bad behavior by their teachers.

The counselor took a set of these students aside and told them that she was going to teach the students how to modify their teachers' behaviors. The students relished the idea of taking control over their teachers by behavioral modification. The counselor explained the **Operant Conditioning** process and told them to react positively whenever the teacher treated them well or offered them the slightest praise; and not to respond, positively or negatively when the teacher was not treating them as well as they wished.

Within weeks, the teacher's negative reports on these students subsided and their grades started to improve.

The students were utilizing Operant Conditioning to modify the behavior of their teachers, but what is more relevant to this section is the fact that the actual use of Operant Conditioning turned out to be a method of modifying their own behaviors — and improving their performance in school.

You need to continually reinforce the habits that you want ingrained in your behavioral patterns. Use the power of repetition. You can decide what behaviors you want reinforced — how you want to be rewarded — and how you want to frame the reward.

You can also reinforce your positive behaviors by actively engaging gratitude with reflection on the positive things that happened at the end of each day. This will lessen the tendency for negative thoughts by increasing melatonin and decreasing cortisol stress hormones in your body. Celebrating creates a dopamine reward for your behaviors and is part of mastering your own Universe.

How To MASTER THE UNIVERSE
Personal and Professional Life-Skills Guide

NLP & NAC Skills

Another branch of psychotherapy that provides a useful methodology for understanding and managing behaviors is called Neuro-Linguistic Programming (NLP). NLP is based on a theory that people are programed with individual biases towards processing visual, auditory, and kinesthetic (physical sensation) information. Leveraging a knowledge of NLP can help you influence behaviors and even detect signs of someone telling the truth from recall or making up answers. Neuro-associative Conditioning (NAC) is an applied practice to leverage NLP to condition and modify your behaviors, and the behaviors of others.

With NLP, people who are more visually biased operate more comfortably in a visual modality with visual cues and phrases such as "the way I see it," or "it looks to me like" — whereas someone with an auditory modality bias might say "it sounds to me" or "I hear what you're saying." Kinesthetically oriented people usually relate better to phrases such as "it seems to me." or "it feels like."

NLP practitioners claim that people have specific eye patterns based on whether they are creating — or if they are recalling information. When creating, problem solving, or thinking of new ideas visually, many people's eyes look to their upper right. When auditorily creating information, such as sounds, spoken words and music, their eyes look to the middle right — towards the ear. When they are creating or thinking kinesthetically — relating to sensations, or feelings — their eyes look to the lower right.

When recalling, or remembering information visually, their eyes usually look to their upper left. When recalling auditorily their eyes look to their middle left and look down to their right if they are either creating or recalling information kinesthetically.

If you are viewing someone else's visual cues, keep in mind that you see them looking to the left when they are looking to their right — and you see them looking to the right when they are looking to their left.

Try to observe your eye motions in these scenarios and determine if you have these, or other eye movement tendencies when creating or recalling different modalities of information.

You can put this information to use towards mastering your Universe. For example, if you have the typical eye patterns described above and are trying to recall an auditory dialog or music, try directing your eyes directly to your right as you recall the information. Or if you are trying to recall visual information, such as an image — try directing your eyes to your upper right as you are trying to recall the information. These techniques may help you recall or create information more easily.

Tony Robbins expanded upon NLP to develop a technique he coined as Neuro-Associative Conditioning, or NAC. NAC involves using behavioral conditioning to associate — or disassociate behaviors with NLP modalities. It is based on the premise that human behavior is primarily driven by the need to avoid pain or the desire to achieve pleasure. Participants are taught to condition desired behaviors by repeatedly associating positive emotions to the behavior, along with their most strongly biased NLP modality — and to condition away undesired behaviors by repeatedly associating negative emotions or experiences with that behavior.

For example, if you want to quit smoking and you have a visual NLP bias, you can condition yourself to visualize a repulsive scene every time you want to smoke to quell your desire to smoke. Likewise, if you want to use NAC to reinforce a behavior, and you have a strongly biased auditory NLP bias, associate your favorite sounds, music, or words with the behavior you want to reinforce.

> The fire walk exercise is used in Tony Robbins seminars as a metaphor for your ability to leverage the sequence and intensity of NLP modalities to conquer your fears and master your behavior. The theory is that you can walk on hot coals if you

follow the same process and intensities as Fijian firewalkers — just as you can bake as good of a cake as a master chef if you add the same ingredients in the same proportions and sequence, bake it for the same length of time, and at the same temperature.

Participants are stirred up to an intensive focus or overload of their auditory and visual NLP modalities to help ignore the kinesthetic effects of hot coals. Participants visually focus ahead and yell "cool moss, cool moss, cool moss" as they walk across the coals. At the end, their feet are washed off to remove any coals that may have stuck to their feet.

I tried it and was able to compete in a volleyball tournament the following evening. Most people — but not everyone completes the exercise without pain or injuries.

NAP can be used to help control your emotions by leveraging the sensory overload technique used in the fire walk exercise. If you are feeling overly emotional and want to control the emotions – try overloading your senses by concentrating on your visual and auditory modes. Look around and focus on sights, whether it's the scenery around you, people, an image in your mind, or even a wall. Listen intently on the sounds around you or music in your head. If you overload your visual and/or auditory modes, you will minimize the impact of your kinesthetic mode.

Even though some of the NLP claims have been difficult to prove, it often helps to pay attention to your NLP biases and the biases of others. You can operate more effectively in your own natural NLP modes of thought and recall, and you can master your interactions with other people more easily if you pay attention to their NLP modal biases. In the section on MASTERING OTHER UNIVERSES, I will share some of the amazing results you can achieve by leveraging NLP and NAC and other behavioral modification techniques to master other people's Universes.

You can pursue a variety of books and seminars on NLP and NAC to help identify your visual, auditory, and kinesthetic modal biases. Once you identify your recall bias, you can leverage that mode to recall information more easily.

Mind over Matter

On January 15, 2009, shortly after takeoff in New York, a flock of geese collided with a passenger airliner and the two engines lost power. Being unable to reach the nearest runway, Captain "Sully" Sullenberger decided that the most viable option was to attempt an emergency landing on the Hudson River.

"I'm sure that my blood pressure and pulse spiked" said Captain Sullenberger, "but I also knew I had to concentrate on the tasks at hand and not let the sensations in my body distract me." When asked if this was difficult, Sully replied "No, it just took some concentration."

In the section on Balance, we mentioned the bilateral relationship between your mental and emotional state and your physiological state. Your mental state can impact your physical state just as your physical state can impact your attitudes and feelings. As in the earlier diving team example, cold weather can make you tighten your shoulders, shiver, and breathe quickly.

Conversely holding your physiology as if you were warm — relaxing your shoulders and breathing slowly in cold weather can make you feel warmer. Relaxed, mindful breathing techniques can also relax your brain and help your mind operate more effectively. Breathing as if you are calm will help you become calm. If you are calm, you can achieve a state of relaxed focus to concentrate on your tasks and challenges.

Try forming the biggest, silliest smile on your face possible. It is difficult to think of depressing thoughts while holding that expression. This is an example of overloading a kinesthetic mode to help master your emotions.

You can think of your Spirit, where your brain and mind mesh together, as your control room to guide your actions towards satisfying the appropriate needs levels required to survive and thrive in Maslow's Hierarchy of Needs.

Uniqueness

Our behaviors are influenced by numerous factors such as our genetic makeup and our reinforced habits — our nature and our nurture. Your soul/mind's makeup has been influenced by events and decisions in your lifetime. If you believe in reincarnation, your soul/mind may have even been influenced by events and decisions in past lives. Your brain and physical makeup are influenced by millions of years of evolutionary factors along with the more recent influences of your environment and specific, inherited genetic traits. There are billions of permutations of these variables in the world, just as there are billions of people in the world. The wide diversity of our personal make-ups helps explain why people can behave and react in such diverse ways — and why it may take different strategies to master our respective Universes.

Some people are naturally wired to take risks. Others are wired for the cautious mitigation of risks. Some prefer flexibility and others need predictability. Some are driven by logic. Others by intuition. Some people need to figure out things on their own and others prefer to be provided predictable directions. Each of these behavioral variations have strengths and weaknesses. From a personal perspective, if you learn how to leverage your strengths, it will be easier for you to achieve your optimal performance. If you stray too far from your natural operating modes, you can run the risk of creating stress and illnesses, even to the point of death — as in the example of a stress related heart attack.

There are many behavioral assessment tools to help understand personality and behavior differences. Your awareness of behavioral differences can be leveraged towards mastering your — and other people's Universes. The tools are typically derived from observed assessments by others and/or self-assessments.

The tools that categorize personality types derived from observed behaviors or personality traits which are typically obtained from questionnaires filled out by colleges or acquaintances. Other self-assessment tools derive their results from self-evaluation questionnaires — and focus more on the underlying drives that motivate our behaviors, rather than the outwardly observed behaviors themselves. This type of assessment tool focuses more on why someone behaves the way they do instead of their surface behaviors.

Both approaches are prone to biases and inconsistencies. Both types of tools typically provide recommendations for leveraging your strengths and mitigating your weakness, as well as strategies to interact more effectively with other behavioral types of people.

This section is intended as an introduction to exploring your natural behavioral wiring. Try out one or more of these tools to learn more about how to optimize your own personal performance.

Personal Mastery

You have the power to master your body and behaviors. You just need to use your mind to apply **THE FORMULA**

(OO + RRR + AA) to the techniques we covered in this section. Decide what you want to accomplish, consider your potential reactions, then act and assess your outcomes to improve your future outcomes.

> **COTU Principle:** Every entity is the Center of its own Universe and is motivated by its own survival and success.

Humans have an amazing power of self-healing.

> "Dr. Richard Mollica of Harvard Medical School's Program in Refugee Trauma has traveled the world working with patients who have been traumatized and physically paralyzed from psychological damage. He has worked with survivors of massacres in Bosnia, genocide in Rwanda, and the 9-11 World Trade Center attack. He insists that he has never met a person without the capacity to overcome suffering. "Never a hopeless patient. Never. And I don't say this lightly." There is a self-healing force inside all human beings "to restore our physical and mental selves to a state of full productivity and quality of life, no matter how severe the initial damage.""
> *The Survivors Club*, By Ben Sherwood (1964-)

Whether your objective at a given time is to survive or thrive, it is much easier to achieve the objective if you break down the challenge into component pieces — then apply **THE FORMULA (OO + RRR + AA)** to the component parts — one at a time. Start with breathing and apply mindfulness techniques to focus and progress through the components of the challenge. The scope of the overall challenge may seem daunting, but the component parts can be easily mastered. Computational problem solving involves decomposition (breaking problems into components), pattern recognition (identifying trends) and establishing algorithms (repeatable processes for solving repetitive problems).

II. MASTERING YOUR UNIVERSE

"How do you eat an elephant? One bite at a time."
African Proverb

Do not just read the words in **THE FORMULA**. Stop and utilize Engaged Thinking and Operant Conditioning to program your behavior. Take the time to determine your objectives. Learn from the results of your actions and adjust your future behaviors based on what you have learned.

You have the power of mind over matter. This section of the book has provided multiple techniques to harness the power of your mind over your brain matter and the power to harness your mind over your body matter. You cannot change what has happened in the past, but you can control how you react or respond to it — and learn from the experience. In the next section I will provide techniques for you to have more power over other entities that you interact with in your Universe.

"Nothing is impossible. The word itself says, 'I'm possible!'"
Audrey Hepburn (1929-*1993*), Actress and Humanitarian

If you want to Master the Universe — follow The Wisdom Way

Mastering the Universe is a journey and not a destination. Destinations are endpoints — and endpoints have no future.

Embrace the destinations — and then move on to enjoy the journey.

How To MASTER THE UNIVERSE
Personal and Professional Life-Skills Guide

III. MASTERING OTHER UNIVERSES

Every other entity is the **Center of their Universe** too — driven by their own survival and success.

Everyone thinks that they are special. And they are!

They are the most important entity in their own Universes. From their perspectives, each of them is the **Center of the Universe**. Even when they have children, the children often become extensions of their internal core — a legacy of their existence — and a potential fulfillment of their ambitions.

Of course, the children become new centers of their Universes too — where the parents start playing supporting roles. As they first enter the physical world, their Universe is consumed with satisfying the basic survival needs in Maslow's Pyramid — breathing, drinking, eating, sleeping, and the other bodily functions. As they mature and evolve, they become aware of other people and the rest of the world — their interdependencies with other Universes to satisfy these basic needs — and then the more evolved needs as they move up the hierarchy of needs. Remember the **COTU Principle**:

> **COTU Principle:** Every entity is the Center of its own Universe and is motivated by its own survival and success.

The world we are living in is filled with other Universes — and subsets of these Universes intersect with your Universe. There are some Universes that you can impact directly, and others that you can impact indirectly. Each of these Universes has its own set of rules, expectations, and agendas — and these parameters can change over time. Keep in mind that we only play supporting roles in other Universes. Dealing with other people, animals, and organizations with the understanding that they are their own centers of their Universes is one of the keys to successfully mastering other Universes.

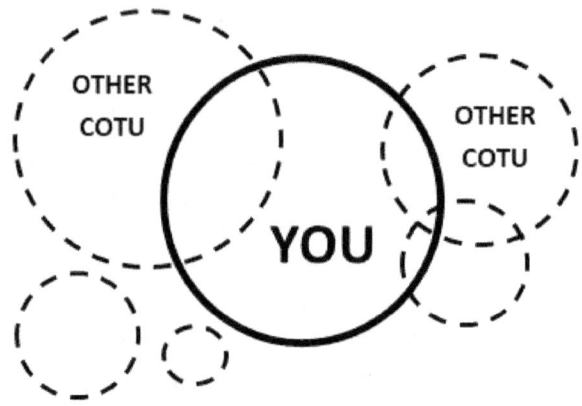

Diversity

"By nature, all men are equal in liberty, but not in other endowments."
Thomas Aquinas (1225-1274), Philosopher and Theologian

We are not all created equally — and this is great news! If we were all the same, we would be living in a very boring world. There is a distinction between "created equally" and being "treated equally." Ideally, we would all be afforded fair and equal opportunities based on past actions and our abilities — even though we are all quite unique and different.

III. MASTERING OTHER UNIVERSES

> "People who look down on other people don't end up being looked up to."
> Robert Half, (1919-2001), Founder of Employment Agency

We all come from and live in our own, different Universes. We have different histories, genetics, and behavioral wiring. A key to mastering your relationship with other people and entities is to elevate your awareness to the next level of consciousness, by trying to understand the world from the perspective of their Universe. After all, they are the respective Centers of their Universes.

> "We are all special cases."
> Albert Camus (1913-1960), Philosopher and Author

Knowing yourself is different from knowing someone else, so "Doing unto others as you would like to have done to you" can be a hit or miss influence strategy. The axiom can work well if the other person is wired like you and has the same personal dynamics and external influences going on at a given time. Otherwise, you are just rolling the dice. To be effective at influencing others, you need to try to do to them as they would like to have done to themselves — at that given time.

Master The Universe Formula
THE FORMULA = OO + RRR + AA

1. **OO** – Determine your Objectives and Options.
2. **RRR** – Consider potential Results, Reactions, and Rewards to determine your course of action.
3. **AA** – Act and Assess.

PRO TIP: Use the condensed acronym **"ORA"** to remember **THE FORMULA.**

If you rely solely on your Reflexive Thinking process — it can be natural to assume that their motivations and potential reactions would be the same as yours. Try to take the time to leverage your Engaged Thinking process to consider how they might react based on past experiences with them or others. It may sound simple, but a lot of people struggle with their own self-awareness in the first step and what they want to accomplish with their interactions. It takes an extra effort to try to understand the perspective of the other party. It takes practice.

Think about these steps when you wake up in the morning and try to practice them every day at least once a day. Then, expand this practice to every interaction. It may take a while to condition yourself to think and act at this level of awareness, but you can master it through repetition. Through repetition, you can naturally ingrain this practice into your everyday life and be deeply rewarded.

> I used to have weekly updates and planning meetings with a manager of mine. He often asked me to think about an idea or topic. I had usually already thought about the topic and, in my first few meetings with him, I would respond quickly.
>
> I noticed that he seemed perplexed and annoyed when I responded so quickly. I realized that in his universe, people need to take more time to think things through.
>
> I thought through my objectives and options — and started telling him that I would think about his questions and get back to him at our next weekly meeting. Even though I usually gave him the same answer the next week as I would have given him on the spot, he was much more receptive to the same answer a week later.

A straightforward way to assess someone's potential reactions is to simply ask the other party directly about their objectives and expectations. You can also share your objectives and expectations to identify potential commonality of intent — or to identify the gaps that need to

III. MASTERING OTHER UNIVERSES

be considered. You can then ask the other party what approach would work best for them to accomplish their objectives and try to discover compatible or mutually agreeable approaches. Finally, brainstorm on a plan of Action and set metrics for satisfying your respective objectives.

> "First seek to understand, then seek to be understood."
> Stephen R. Covey (1932-) author and motivational speaker

Relationships

SOUL-MATE MODEL

```
        ┌─────────────┐
        │    SOUL     │
        │      ┌──────┼──┐
        │      │ MIND │  │
    ┌───┼──────┤SPIRIT│  │
    │   │      │ BRAIN│  │
    │   └──────┤      │  │
    │  SOUL    │   BODY  │
    │     ┌────┼─┐ └─────┘
    │     │MIND│ │
    │     │SPIRIT│
    │     │BRAIN│ │
    └─────┤     │─┘
          │ BODY│
          └─────┘
```

Some relationships occur on a one-time transactional basis, but many relationships will be built over time with multiple interactions. We are aware of tangible relationships between our bodies and minds via communications in the physical world. These relationships can be built via verbal, visual or other physical communications. It is also possible that our souls have relationships too — possibly over

87

multiple lifetimes or between lifetimes. This would reinforce the concept of having soul mates.

> "When someone has a strong intuitive connection, Buddhism suggests that it's because of karma, some past connection."
> Richard Gere (1949-), Actor

> "Would you know my name if I saw you in heaven?"
> Eric Clapton (1945-), Musician

Relationships can grow and be reinforced through the techniques outlined in this section of the book. Even the concepts of timing and space can be important towards developing relationships.

> "Let there be spaces in your togetherness."
> Kahlil Gibran, (1983-1931), Writer and Philosopher

Open discussions can help strengthen relationships if they are not overdone. Sometimes leaving a little vacuum as described earlier can help pull both parties together.

> "Relationships can be like gardening. It is healthy to pull up plants and inspect their roots occasionally, but if you do it too often you will kill them."
> Harvey Linebarrier (1949-), Sales Professional and Wine Grower

Rapport Skills

According to Maslow's Hierarchy of Needs, we all have requirements to satisfy Social and Self-Esteem Needs to be able to successfully progress to the Self-actualization stage.

III. MASTERING OTHER UNIVERSES

If you focus on how to help others satisfy these needs, you will have an easier time meshing and establishing rapport with them.

The existence of multiple Universes that can overlap with each other can create conflicts and/or create opportunities. Awareness is a key to mastering the overlap, or collisions, between your Universe and other Universes. Many people only think at the basic level of how an interaction has an effect within the awareness of their own Universe. Raising your awareness to also consider the impact on the other entity's Universe can have a profound effect on the personal results you achieve. This applies to interpersonal interactions as well as interactions with organizations, organisms, animals, and other entities.

> "It's nice to be important, but it's more important to be nice."
> Dwayne Johnson (1972-), Actor and
> Professional Wrestler

Do you want to be liked? Respected? Feared? Despised? Are you satisfying your Social and Self-Esteem needs? Are you satisfying the needs of the other party? Decide what you want to accomplish. What people think about you, usually has more to do with how you make them feel about themselves than what you say about yourself. Applying THE FORMULA to this decision process.

> I was once in a car with four passengers when I noticed that one of the passengers was constantly interrupting the other passengers to one-up the topic and talk about him/herself. Out of curiosity, I started counting the number of seconds it took for that person to interrupt another passenger. Having briefly been a wrestling referee when I was in college, I was reasonably good at counting seconds. During a 20-minute period there were only two times when it took more than 5-seconds for that person's interruption and those two pauses only lasted for 7-seconds each.

How To MASTER THE UNIVERSE
Personal and Professional Life-Skills Guide

I suspect that the passenger making the interruptions was trying to impress the other passengers. It had exactly the opposite effect. People usually think less of someone who is constantly interrupting them to shift the attention to themselves. A skilled relationship artist typically focuses on how to make the other people or entities feel better about themselves.

> "One of the many things we have learned in all our travels is that it's the people who count… most people everywhere are interesting, and if you can't find a friend, then maybe there is something wrong with you."
> Barbara Bush (1925-2018), 41st First Lady of the United States

Ask questions and encourage others to spend more time talking about themselves than the time you spend talking about yourself. Ask about their backgrounds, ideas, interests, and opinions.

> My sister was once invited to be part of the welcome party for the, then President and Vice-President of United States. She said that the President smiled, shook her hand, looked into her eyes, and for that brief moment in time he made her feel like she was the total center of his attention — and the most important person in the world.

I have heard similar stories about another former-President. We all have things going on that could distract us from focusing on the people we are interacting with in-the-moment. The POTUS was someone who had the weight of the world's issues on his shoulders, and he was able to focus on the person and situation at that moment. This is a great example of someone who was skilled at focusing on the other person in-the-moment and totally impressing the other person in the process.

III. MASTERING OTHER UNIVERSES

> "Pretend that every single person you meet has a sign around his or her neck that says, "Make me feel important."
> Mary Kay Ash (1918–2001), founder of Mary Kay Cosmetics

Establishing rapport involves learning how to mesh with another party's Universe and finding areas of commonality. Areas of commonality can come in the form of common interests such as vocations, vacations, family similarities, hobbies, sports, infirmities, politics, religions, or other shared experiences.

In a 2019 interview with the *San Francisco Chronicle*, Amaryllis Fox discussed her life when she was the youngest CIA operative. In Fox's book *Life Undercover: Coming of Age in the CIA*, she described an incredible meeting with the leader of an al Qaeda terror cell. It started as a weapons negotiation and somehow ended with the two bonding as parents over pediatric cough remedies.

"When we took off our fighter hats and put on our parent hats, suddenly both of us were parents of children who were affected by asthma and could share in that struggle and in the solutions that we'd found for it.

Those are the opportunities that we all have every day when we find ourselves in a frustrating argument, to just take a step back and identify what it is that we share, rather than digging in our heels. I smile every day when I find myself remembering that lesson."

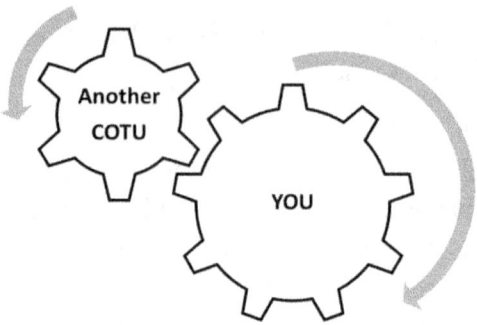

The meshing process can be more subtle and powerful than just sharing commonalities of backgrounds, experiences, and ideas. It can also involve meshing with the other party's gestures, rate of speech, the words they use and even types of words they use. If two gears are not going in a compatible direction, at the same speed, and with compatible cogs, it will be difficult to mesh the gears.

One meshing technique involves pacing and then leading. Pacing and then leading is a technique used in hypnotism as well. Hypnotists often use a countdown of numbers to artificially induce a trace state resembling sleep to create a heightened susceptibility to suggestion. You can often create the same effect through mirroring the other party before attempting to lead them in another direction.

When you mirror another party's behavior and phraseology, it may seem awkward to you because you if you are behaving and using phrases outside of your comfort zone. It turns out that this very behavior and phraseology is comfortable and natural to the other party. If you start mirroring or pacing the other party, it is like meshing two gears together. If someone experiences something familiar, as with mirroring, their mind is put in a state of cognitive ease. Repeating something creates cognitive ease as well — making it even more memorable and persuasive.

Once your gears are synchronized, you can start changing

III. MASTERING OTHER UNIVERSES

the pace and direction of the other gear. I will discuss this further when we explore behavioral modification and NLP with others. These rapport building techniques can apply to your interactions with other entities like animals, organisms, or organizations as well.

If you want to encourage someone to agree with you, try to synchronize with them and then nod positively while you ask a question. Often times, this will trigger them to nod back and agree.

A simple and powerful technique to quickly establish rapport with another person when you first meet, is the TENS technique.

TENS Rapport Technique:

T = **T**ouch (if appropriate).
E = Make **E**ye contact
N = Repeat back their **N**ame one or more times.
    e.g., "Hi Jane, it's nice to meet you."
S = **S**mile!

Pro Tips:
- You do not need to follow these steps in sequential order. The acronym TENS just makes it easier to remember. I usually like to start and end with a smile. Use whatever sequence seems the most natural for the situation.
- The Touch step should be subject to appropriate cultural and health guidelines. You can always substitute another physical acknowledgement like a tap to your heart, a fist-bump, a bow, or a wave in times of a health crisis.
- In times of masking for a pandemic, it may be impossible to see the smile of your mouth unless you are on a video conference. Smiling creates a change in your eye expression that can be seen by the other party — even if they cannot see your mouth.

Example: I used the TENS Rapport Technique to establish rapport with the security guard and clerks in the earlier Laundry Room Dilemma and Reunion Penthouse Suite examples of applying THE FORMULA. I made eye contact and smiled. They smiled back. I asked their names and repeated back their names as I introduced myself. I left out the touching option because it would not have been appropriate in these situations. Using this technique to establish rapport helped me put them in a more relaxed and constructive state of problem solving.

A side benefit from consciously repeating their name is that it will help you remember their name more easily. Also, the very physical act of smiling will make you happier. If you start consciously practicing the TENS Rapport Technique every time you meet someone you can condition yourself to do this automatically and enjoy the benefits of instant rapport.

"Everyone likes a compliment."
Abraham Lincoln (1809-1865), 16th US President

You can also subtly disengage with others by introducing dissimilarities, or gears that do not mesh well with the other person. You can switch to different gestures, rates of speech or NLP modality terms than the other person is using. For instance, if they are more visually oriented, switch to auditory or kinesthetic language.

Authenticity in your interest in the other party's Universe makes a difference too. People can often sense when you are not being authentic.

I helped advise a Tulane University student project to develop tools that can identify whether someone was really experiencing real pain, or just faking it. The goal was to screen drug addicts who

III. MASTERING OTHER UNIVERSES

> were faking pain to obtain opioids. Another advisor was an Emergency Room doctor, who said that he could usually tell if a patient was faking the pain. If the patient opened with trying to befriend the ER doctor, asking questions like how the doctor was doing, etc. — the patient was usually faking pain to obtain the opioids.

If you really try to understand and care about the other party's Universe, you will be more successful at establishing rapport and potentially learn something new from their lens on the world. You can mesh with them by being empathetic to their situation, even if you are not necessarily sympathetic. For instance, you can authentically tell someone that you understand that they are upset even if you do not agree with the reasons why they are upset.

> "To belittle, you have to be little."
> Kahlil Gibran, (1983-1931), Writer and Philosopher

Demonstrate a sincere interest in the other person. Ask them about their favorite activities, what they like about their job, their best vacation, most memorable movies they have seen, the best songs that they have heard, people that they have met, what they like the most about themselves, their claim to fame, and what makes them smile.

> One Friday afternoon, while finishing up a business trip, I was at my hotel waiting for a taxi to take me to the airport. Another car cut off my arriving taxi just as the driver was pulling in to pick me up. When I got in the taxi, the driver was angrily cursing out the car that cut him off.
> I waited for him to pause and then asked him what was going well in his life. He acted surprised with the question, and after a moment he told me about his son getting accepted to college. I probed him further about his son and other children and totally turned his attitude around — and had a very pleasant ride to the airport.

"I've learned that people will forget what you said, people will forget what you did, but people will never forget how you made them feel."
Maya Angelou (1928-) American author and poet.

Smiling

It takes 72 muscles to frown and 14 to smile.

Smiling is easy — and it is contagious. People have a subconscious tendency to match other people's emotions. If your smile appears authentic, it compels others to like you — which is why it is part of the TENS Rapport technique.

Studies by UCLA Professor, Dr. Albert Mehrabian have demonstrated that 93 percent of communications are nonverbal. They are 55 percent visual, 38 percent vocal (tonal and inflections) and only 7 percent verbal. Your body language, posture and smiles make a profound difference in your communications.

UC Berkely psychologists Dacher Keltner, PhD and Lee Anne Harker, PhD compared yearbook photos of 21-year-old graduates and found that the ones who appeared to have genuinely positive smiles had healthier marriages when they were 52 years old.

Smiles make you and others happier and healthier. The act of smiling triggers your Reactive Thinking into perceiving an absence of threats, which slows down your heart rate, reduces the production of the stress hormone cortisol, and smiling can reduce your blood pressure. Smiling generates endorphins in our systems, which make us feel better by reducing the perception of pain in our brains. Even forcing a smile can relax your heart rate and reduce stress according to a study at the University of Kansas.

> A Japanese man with a sweet tooth who believes in smiles has become the world's oldest male at 112 years and 344 days old, according to *Guinness World Records*. Chitetsu Watanabe, who was born in Niigata in northern Japan in 1907, received a certificate for his accomplishment on Wednesday at a nursing home in the city. Asked about the secret to longevity, Watanabe has this advice: Don't get angry and keep smiling.
> February 2020.

Smiling is a physical act that positively impacts your emotional attitude in the manner that we discussed in the section on Mind over Matter. Happiness makes us smile — and smiling makes us happier. Smiling is a natural behavior and not simply a learned behavior. Studies have demonstrated that even blind children smile when they are happy even though they have not had the benefit of learning from observing others.

> "If you see someone without a smile today, give 'em yours."
> Dolly Parton (1946-), Singer, Songwriter and Actress

Probing & Listening Skills

> "Judge a man by his questions rather than his answers."
> Voltaire (1694-1778), French Author

The use of open-ended questions is a technique used by interviewers and salespeople to gather more thorough information. An open-ended question is a question that is not easily answered with a yes or no response. Questions that can be answered with a yes, no, or one-word response are called close-ended questions.

Examples of open-ended questions are ones that include

words like "what," "when," "where," and "why." Closed-ended questions often include words like "are" and "is." An open-ended question usually requires more detailed and interesting responses to the questions. An example of using an open-ended question instead of a closed-ended question is asking "What did you think about the speech" — instead of asking a closed-ended question like "Did you like the speech?" The former question makes the other person think and explain their perspective on the situation instead of just responding yes or no.

> "My greatest strength as a consultant is to be ignorant and ask a few questions."
> Peter Drucker (1909 – 2005), Management Consultant

Deep Probing involves asking second, third and sometimes deeper levels of open-ended questions, such as "**Why** do you think that way about the situation?" and then "**How** do you think the situation affects you," followed by "**What** would you do differently?" The deeper you can probe, the better you can understand the other person — the more you can respect their perspective of being the Center of the Universe — and the easier it will be to establish rapport. Second and third level open-ended questioning is a good follow-on to the TENS Technique for establishing deeper rapport. Deep Probing though the first and second steps of **THE FORMULA (OO + RRR + AA)** can provide a sound foundation for a consulting practice too.

> "I never learned anything when I was talking."
> Larry King (1933-2021), Radio and television host.

You need to develop good listening skills if you really want to benefit from effective probing. In fact, you will become more proficient at Mastering the Universe if you learn to listen more effectively — whether you are probing

III. MASTERING OTHER UNIVERSES

or not.

> "We have two ears and one mouth so that we can listen twice as much as we speak."
> Epictetus (55–135 AD), Philosopher

> When I am a participant in an interactive meeting, I have learned that sometimes the less often I talk, the smarter the others think I am. They are correct too. By listening to others, I am learning from their perspectives and have more time to formulate better quality contributions to the meeting.

There is a difference between hearing and listening. Hearing is done with your body and listening is accomplished by engaging your mind to pay attention to what you are hearing. Listening involves hearing what the other party is trying to tell you and learning from what you hear. Hearing is more of a Reflexive Thinking process, and you can listen more effectively if you take the time and effort to employ Engaged Thinking.

> **Hear:** to be aware of sounds with your ears
> **Listen:** take notice of and act on what someone says
> *Oxford Dictionary*

Space and timing are important for effective probing and listening. When you ask a question — shut up! Give the other person space to think about your question — and give them time to answer your question. Space in a conversation creates a vacuum that people feel compelled to fill. If you jump in and try to fill in their answer for them, you might not really find out what they are thinking. Also, they will likely be annoyed that you did not really care enough about their answer to give them the space to respond.

> "Be curious, not judgmental."
> Walt Whitman (1819-1892), American Poet

Restraint

"The art of conversation is not only to say the right thing at the right time, but also to leave unsaid, the wrong thing at the most tempting moment."
Dee Tenorio, Romance Novelist

What you do not say is often more impactful than what you do say. Think about the potential consequences of reacting now versus waiting to respond in the future. You may decide to delay your comments and questions until a more opportune moment — decide to reserve the comments for another party — or decide to leave your thoughts to yourself altogether. Remember that with Operant Conditioning, not responding is a technique to avoid reinforcing an undesired behavior. Reacting quickly is usually a consequence of Reflexive Thinking whereas a considered response involves Engaged Thinking.

> I had a teacher in high school that used to ask the class a question and then call on someone for an answer, who did not have their hand raised. He would berate the student for not knowing the answer. So, I decided to stop raising my hand — even if I thought that I knew the correct answer. There was no benefit to raising my hand. I was more likely to be called upon if I did not raise my hand. Also, I concluded that you learn more from listening than you do from talking.
> One day, he asked a question, and no one raised their hands to answer. I knew the answer but did not raise my hand either. The teacher started complaining about "students these days" not bothering to study their materials and asked why no one was raising their hands.
> I calmly replied that no one was raising their hands because he always called on students who did not have their hands raised. This infuriated him even more and he angrily asked if I was questioning

III. MASTERING OTHER UNIVERSES

his teaching methods — to which I responded no and that I was only answering his question.

If someone does something that you consider to be stupid — how do you react? Do you tell them that they are stupid? If you do, how do you think that they will react? Are they more likely to respect you for your comment? Will they be motivated to change their behaviors — or to get defensive and react negatively?

In the anecdote about the high school teacher, I may have won the admiration of other students, but I probably lost points with the teacher. If my objective was to get better grades, I could have either kept my mouth shut, or maybe constructively talked with the teacher about this after class.

Two secrets of success are:
1. Don't tell people everything you know.

This adage also applies to confidentiality. You may hear observe or hear things that are better off not speaking about, either to the person involved or to others. Think carefully about the consequences of spreading gossip. Try applying **THE FORMULA** to think through the impact of disseminating sensitive information. If your objective is to draw short-term attention to yourself, you might achieve your goal — but at what cost? Think about the reactions you might provoke in others. The person you are talking about may resent you and never trust you again. Also, you are sending a message to others that you cannot be trusted with anyone's private information. If you choose the option to remain silent, one of the long-term benefits is that people will share more information with you — and knowledge can be power.

Never lie, but don't always blab the truth.

If someone else is trying to make a point, it is often worth taking the time to probe further to make sure you understand their position. You typically appear more credible if you research the topic further before commenting. It is powerful to say something like "I never thought of it that way" or "let me think about it and get back to you." The other person will feel more respected, and this will provide you with time for a more thoughtful response. It might even change your mind on the topic. As discussed in the section on listening, pausing to create space in the conversation will create that vacuum that the other person will feel compelled to fill.

Be conscious of the timing of the development of a relationship and avoid pushing too quickly or too hard — until your gears are in synch. The vacuum you create acts similar to a vacuum in physical space where molecules are compelled to spread into — and to fill the void. It is also analogous to creating a magnetic field that attracts the other party — in the process creating a more "magnetic personality" for yourself.

There are also times when you would be remised to remain silent. If you are observing a social injustice, not speaking out decisively is tantamount to supporting the action.

> "If I were to remain silent, I'd be guilty of complicity."
> Albert Einstein (1879-1955), Theoretical Physicist

Take the time to leverage your Engaged Thinking process and apply **THE FORMULA (OO + RRR + AA)**. What is your objective and what kind of reactions would you anticipate if you react now, if you react later — or if you keep your reactions to yourself? You have the ability to master the timing of your actions and your impact upon others.

III. MASTERING OTHER UNIVERSES

Interactive Behavioral Modification

The Classical and Operant Behavior Modification techniques we discussed in Section 2 can be applied to repetitive interactions with others. You can use the Stimulus-Response (S-R) conditioning pattern of Classical Conditioning, as with the Pavlov's Dog example, for conditioning basic reflexive behaviors in others. Keep in mind that there is a limited conditioning effect once you remove the substitute stimulus.

You can use Operant Conditioning to condition more complex behavioral patterns in others. The example in **Section 2** where students were taught how to condition their teacher's behavior was a good example of intentionally modifying their teacher's behavior based on how the teacher expected the students to react.

You can see this effect on service people. If a waitperson, clerk, customer service, or salesperson starts getting a series of negative reactions from customers, they can be conditioned to have a negative attitude towards customers. By having a negative attitude in anticipation to negative reactions, they will likely create more dissatisfied, negative customers — which will further reinforce their negative attitudes. This creates a negative Vicious Cycle of Operant Conditioning.

Conversely, if the service person gets accustomed to positive reactions from customers, the service person is more likely to have a positive attitude. That positive attitude will likely be positively reinforced by positive reactions from customers in the future. This creates a positive Virtuous Cycle of Operant Conditioning.

You can take control of the Operant Conditioning by thinking through **THE FORMULA (OO + RRR + AA)** and applying it to how you master the reactions of others.

> As a young salesperson, I was once discussing an extremely difficult customer with my sales

manager. My sales manager said that he could tell how much I disliked this customer based on my voice and facial expressions. I thought about it and realized that my attitude probably came through to the customer as well, which in turn, reinforced his difficult behavior with me.

From then on, I decided to be happy and excited whenever I talked with the customer. At first, the customer acted confused by my change in behavior, but he gradually became much friendlier and easy to work with. And I ended up closing a deal with this customer that was the largest deal of the year in the region.

In this example, I determined that my objective was to get this difficult customer to work with me in a more positive and constructive manner. To accomplish this, I repetitively used Operant Conditioning to positively reinforce the reactions I wanted to achieve from the customer.

Operant Conditioning with positive reinforcement can reinforce positive behaviors, and you can sometimes eliminate negative behaviors by not reacting or reinforce the behaviors that you would like to end. In the previous sales example, whenever the customer reacted negatively, I did not get upset or otherwise react to his negative behavior. Instead, I focused on reinforcing his positive behavior whenever it occurred — and eventually he stopped acting negatively.

> If you nod and smile when you ask a question, the other person is more likely to agree and respond positively.

For extreme situations, negative reinforcement can be a stronger method of conditioning behavior than positive reinforcement. It can send a clear message that there is a penalty for undesirable behavior. Once burned, people learn quickly to avoid touching a hot grill.

III. MASTERING OTHER UNIVERSES

They say that it only takes one lesson to learn how to wrestle an alligator. It is a pass/fail class.

You can apply the same Operant Conditioning techniques to master your relationships with customers, colleagues, friends, family – and even strangers. Keep in mind that we are all unique and wired differently, and part of their wiring comes from conditioning they have had from interactions with other people. You may have to modify your approach as you assess their personality types and their reactions. The more their behavior has been programed from past reactions, the more repetition it may take to change their behavior patterns.

Influencing with NLP

Another approach to conditioning someone else's behavior is to make the effort to identify and appeal to their NLP biases — visual, auditory, or kinesthetic modes of creating and recalling information. A person's bias towards one mode for creating ideas may be different from their mode for recalling information. For example, one person might give visual cues as to when they are making up an answer to a question versus kinesthetic cues when remembering an answer. Another person might give auditory cues when they are making up the answer and visual cues when they are answering from their memory. A person's que can come in the form of the language they use or other cues such as their eye movements described in the NLP/NAC explanation in **Section 2**. If you can recognize a person's cues, they can give you a clue as to whether the person is telling the truth or lying.

Recognizing a person's NLP biases can make it easier to mesh and establish rapport. If someone uses auditory language, and you speak with them with auditory terms that they are comfortable with, it will be easier to mesh with their gears. If they use kinesthetic or visual language, then use kinesthetic or visual language.

You can also add similar pacing to your conversation. If they speak slowly — then start out speaking slowly. If they speak quickly, then start out speaking quickly. If they use wide gestures with their hands, then start out using wide gestures with your hands.

You may think that it sounds or looks odd, it is only because it may be different than your normal comfort zone — but to them, it will seem like a more natural and comfortable conversation. If you think back on the discussion on thinking processes in **Section 1**, the repetition of the terminology is helping put them in a state of cognitive ease — which makes it more memorable and persuasive. Once you have effectively paced their language and behaviors, it will be easier to adjust and lead the interaction.

There have been debates regarding the ethics behind employing behavioral modification techniques such as pacing and leading, Operant Conditioning, Classical Conditioning, NLP, and NAC. It often comes down to the underlying intent of the practitioner. If the intent is to maliciously manipulate the other party, then the ethics of the practice can come into question. On the other hand, if the intent is to create a positive outcome, the practitioner is making an extra effort to understand and adjust to the other party's Universe.

Setting Expectations

The success or failure of a relationship is highly dependent on the expectations you establish. This applies to your expectations and the other party's expectations. The expectations can be an outcome of applying the first step of **The Formula** — determining the Objectives and Options for an interaction or relationship. Probing and coming to a verbal agreement can help clarify each party's expectations.

III. MASTERING OTHER UNIVERSES

For more complex interactions it helps to capture the expectations in writing and even review each other's understanding of the expectations for clarification.

It is easier to sell expectations than it is to sell excuses.

A good strategy when making commitments is to under-commit rather than to under-perform. An exception to this rule which is sometimes used as a marketing strategy is to make a "Big Fat Claim" to get people's attention. If you do, be prepared to fulfill the claim if you want to build and maintain a long-term relationship with the other parties.

Conflicts

THE FORMULA (OO + RRR + AA) uses the word "consider" in the following steps to master a Universe rather than simply complying with the other party's objectives. You can consider the other party's objectives without agreeing or complying with their objectives. It is usually best if you can find a way to satisfy both or your objectives with a win/win outcome, but this is not always possible. If you want to more effectively **Master the Universe**, make it your decision as to how you want to act.

Master The Universe Formula
THE FORMULA = OO + RRR + AA

1. **OO** – Determine your Objectives and Options.
2. **RRR** – Consider potential Results, Reactions, and Rewards to determine your course of action.
3. **AA** – Act and Assess.
   PRO TIP: Use the condensed acronym **"ORA"** to remember **THE FORMULA**.

Try to qualify the other party's objectives before jumping to conclusions. The better you understand the priorities from the perspective of their Universe, the better you can decide how to act. You might be rewarded with a new perspective that is better than the one you were originally holding. If you can accommodate the objectives of the other party's Universe while achieving your objectives, you might be able to turn the potential conflict into a win/win situation.

People's positions can stem from rational or from emotional responses. Sometimes logic and facts will prevail, but other times conflicts require a more nuanced approach to address emotional and physical needs.

Relating back to Maslow's Pyramid, behaviors are driven by safety, social and self-esteem needs. Humans have a built-in herd instinct to achieve safety in numbers. The greater the number of people in the group, the more a person is driven to conform to the group. They also have social, and self-esteem needs for acceptance by others. This can drive them to accept falsehoods that appear to defy logic. Many people will naturally defer to be wrong with a group than to think through being right on their own.

Fortunately, you have a choice. You can decide if you want to be an independent thinker or a herd follower.

Directly challenging a person's beliefs stimulates an emotional defense mechanism triggered from a part of the brain called the amygdala. The amygdala sends signals to the sympathetic nervous system to create a fight or flight response. Pushing a position that threatens someone's basic needs and defense systems can make them even more defensive.

Keep in mind that we are all susceptible to reflexive reactions such as these — driven by our basic needs. You can master these situations by training your mind to use **THE FORMULA** to override your brain – switching from your Reflexive Thinking to your Engaged Thinking process. In effect, using your mind over your brain matter.

One technique towards winning an argument is using **The Counterproposal Paradox**. This is when you present an extreme alternative to a position that makes it difficult for them to disagree with your point of view. If you do not do "X," then "Y" will happen. The danger with this approach is that it might trigger the other party's defense mechanisms. Conversely, be aware that the other party might try using this technique on you.

A diplomatic approach to deal with conflicting positions is to change the situation into a joint problem-solving initiative. This approach can stimulate collaboration by appealing to social and self-esteem needs. It helps to discuss and agree to some basic "Rules of Engagement" at the start, such as searching for areas of commonality, not interrupting each other, letting the other party speak after a set amount of time, and not insulting each other or making it personal.

Try to agree on mutuality of intent — a shared interest in uncovering the facts or at least understanding each other's positions. If someone says that we should do "X," you can explore their objectives — you can ask them why they want to do "X." Ask questions about their sources and how they came to their positions — and share your process. Try to make it non-confrontational and identify common objectives and shared positions before exploring differences of opinion. Tell the other party that you agree with them, whenever you uncover common positions or objectives.

Transition your Objective from winning an argument — to sharing, learning, and creating an opportunity to move forward with the other person. You can ask if they have any ideas on alternatives that might accomplish the common objectives and suggest some yourself to discover if there is a more mutually acceptable solution. Listen to the other person and be willing to consider altering your position too.

> The philosophy of Jiu-jitsu is usually more effective than Karate in resolving non-physical conflicts. Karate counteracts force with force, whereas Jiu-jitsu harnesses a force in the direction that it is flowing and then redirects it onto a different path.

There may be times when the interests of the other party are at odds with yours. You may be dealing with a party you do not respect, an enemy, a sports or game opponent, or a party that just happens to have a different objective than you have at that time. There are some people and Universes that may be incompatible or contrary to your values and beliefs, such as unethical or criminal endeavors. Try to identify these situations as early as possible and decide if you can avoid them completely.

If their objectives are still different than yours and you cannot avoid it, you can take actions to disrupt their Universe. There may be situations where you are left with no option other than fighting back.

The **COTU Principle** states that entities are driven to survive and thrive. As with Maslow's Hierarchy of Needs, you need to survive before you can thrive.

There are alternative forces that you may be able to utilize to overcome violence. In **Section 1** we mentioned Alvin Toffler's book *Powershift*, where he describes the relationships between three types of power: Knowledge, Wealth, and Violence. Violence or physical force can be used to acquire Wealth by using physical force or armies to take land or money from others. Conversely, Wealth can be used to acquire instruments of Violence such as weapons and armies. There usually involves a binary exchange of Violence for Wealth, or the other way around. It is typically a win/lose transaction. Knowledge turns out to be the most powerful instrument of power because it can be used to acquire Wealth or Violence — and Knowledge can add upon itself. If two entities exchange Knowledge, they can both end up with more Knowledge.

Leveraging the concepts of space and timing can also make a considerable difference towards resolving conflicts.

> In James Clavell's epic novel *Shogun*, the Japanese commander Lord Toranaga kept his distance and delayed an engagement with a much

III. MASTERING OTHER UNIVERSES

larger army until a natural disaster occurred that turned the odds into his favor.

You can avoid rushing into a conflict if you can take the time to chart out a more productive approach. Sometimes conflict is unavoidable, but taking a collaborative approach often achieves better results for all parties.

Winning

Do you want to be right, or do you want to win?

The better question is "do you want to be both right and win as well?" It can be easy to be right and to lose. The more rewarding challenge is figuring out how to be right and to win. Sometimes the winning can come at a future time based on how well you have considered both your and the other party's Objectives, potential Rewards and Reactions before you choose your Action.

> I was looking forward to enjoying myself last New Year's Eve, but my wife was upset with me about something — and I did not think was "right" for her to be upset over the issue. Explaining my logic on the matter was not working so I decided to test out **THE FORMULA**.
> I considered options such as arguing the logic or using sarcasm but decided that these options would sabotage my objective of enjoying the evening. So, I decided to let her cool off while I enjoyed watching a football game — and then went to her and started kissing her face until she couldn't help but start laughing.
> We both "won" and had an enjoyable evening. And we won without worrying about who was "right." Granted, this option would not be appropriate in most situations, but it was a good test of **THE FORMULA.**

If a supervisor recommends a course of action that you think is stupid, you could tell the supervisor that the action is stupid and possibly be right — but this would likely be a losing proposition for you. It would be more effective to turn it into a joint brainstorming session by using Deep Probing to understand their Objectives and potential Results. Try Consider their opinions with and open mind. Then jointly explore alternative Options towards achieving the goals.

> "Tact is the art of making a point without making an enemy."
> Sir Isaac Newton (1643 – 1727)

Another method of winning is to change the game. Game theory experts claim that there are only five ways that you can change a game. You can combine several of these methods and introduce them at different strategic points in the interaction.

P-A-R-T-S – Game Changing Techniques:

1. **P**layers – Depending on your objectives you can change the participants on your team; add allies or partners to strengthen your advantage; or introduce competitive players to distract your opponent or dilute the playing field. You can also decide to partner with the other player instead of competing.
2. **A**dded Value – Price is not the only value to a negotiation. In business, you can also introduce other values such as the enticement of future business, referrals, press releases, joining forces against common competitors, cross-purchasing agreements, establishing standards to increase the addressable market, joint supplier benefits, most-favored-customer clauses, payment terms, and/or exclusivity rights. And perceived value often supersedes tangible value.

III. MASTERING OTHER UNIVERSES

3. **R**ules – Change the rules to your benefit or follow more unexpected rules than your opponent. Rules provide a structure for how the game will be played. There may be perceived, written, or verbally agreed rules, but players can often remake the rules to their advantage.
4. **T**actics – You can change your actions if your current approach is not achieving your strategic objectives. Consider the other party's potential perceptions of your actions, how they are reacting to your tactics and how you can improve your approach. You can also change tactics to disrupt the other party's rhythm and expectations.
5. **S**cope – Change the size of the playing field to one which provides you with the best advantage. Games are often linked to other games or interdependencies. You can change the scope by adding or reducing other components to the negotiation, such as more or less value exchanging hands, the inclusion of other partners, geographic or market boundaries.

In the 1990's, the computer company Sun Microsystems wanted to gain an advantage over its competitors by having a processor designed to optimize the performance of its operating system.

At the time, computer companies awarded the contract to build their processors to one company. Sun went out to bid with several processor chip manufacturers and ended up selecting, not one, but three companies to produce processor chips for them. With this approach, the suppliers would constantly be competing on the price, quality, and performance of their processors.

One of the Japanese companies said that they never expected the contract to be awarded to more than one of the companies — and never thought to ask because it had never been done before.

Sun became the second largest computer company in the world. One of the reasons was from their willingness to "think outside the box" and change the game. In this situation they applied several if the **P-A-R-T-S** techniques — all without compromising their ethics or integrity.

Another example of changing tactics in a conflict is described in the *Book of 5 Rings*. When a sword fighter establishes a rhythm of certain repetitive sword fighting maneuvers, they can surprise the opponent with an unexpected maneuver that leads to a victory.

Think about what winning means to you and what winning would look like. Why do you want to win — and what are you willing to trade in return? Try to find participants with compatible goals and pursue win/win scenarios and see if you can identify a winning scenario for all parties?

> It is usually easier to win with others than winning by yourself.

Judgmentalism

> Assumptions are the bane of good judgement.

We mentioned before that assumptions are often a consequence of Reflexive Thinking that help your thought process to flow more efficiently. We identify pattern recognitions from previous experiences and our reactions have been conditioned to use a speedy thought process instead of taking the time and effort required for an Engaged Thinking process.

> If a barking dog chases you, it would be fair to assume that you should react with a fight or flight response.

When you become judgmental by making assumptions about people and their intentions, you run the risk of making mistakes. People are wired differently based on their nature and their past experiences. Most people have good intentions based on their past experiences, but their behaviors may be different than what you would expect, based on how they are wired. If they are wired to delegate and you are wired to be hands on, their behaviors will be different than yours. If they are wired to be a risk taker and you are wired to be cautious, your behaviors will be different. Influences such as different religious or cultural beliefs may affect their behaviors differently than yours, even though you may have similar intentions.

> "It's unseemly to criticize without knowledge."
> James Clavell (1921-1994), Novelist

You may be unaware of situational dynamics that are driving unexpected behaviors in others. For example, if someone is driving wildly and cuts you off in traffic, you do not really know if that person is being a jerk or if they have a medical emergency that necessitates their aggressive behavior.

Be open to testing your assumptions. If you can talk with the other person, you can use your probing skills to ask and assess their intentions — and open a new opportunity to learn from the other party. Then you can apply **THE FORMULA** to try to understand the other party's potential Reactions and Rewards.

> "Do not judge others. Be your own judge and you will be truly happy. If you try to judge others, you are likely to burn your fingers."
> Mahatma Gandhi (1869-1948), Indian Civil Rights Leader

Forgiveness

Forgiveness can be admirable and constructive — especially combined with acceptance and wisdom. You cannot change the past, but you can learn from it and change how you react to it. You can linger on an incident and let it extend its negative impact on you — or you can take control and leverage the situation to improve future encounters.

> "Darkness cannot drive out darkness; only light can do that. Hate cannot drive out hate; only love can do that."
> Martin Luther King, Jr. (1957-1968), Minister and Activist

If you believe that another party has wronged you, consider the situation from the other party's perspective. It may have been appropriate behavior for them to achieve their objectives or their behavior may have come from situational conditioning. For example, with Operant Conditioning, a behavior is trained by anticipated responses to a behavior. Maybe other parties have conditioned them to behave as they did to you. Or they may have made a mistake that can be turned into a learning opportunity. At other times, the other party might just be a bad actor that you should try to avoid in the future.

> "Too often people think of courage in terms of not backing down from a fight. I believe that it takes courage to apologize or admit a wrong. I encourage them to not let their anger lead them into self-destruction."
> "I grew, matured and became a person of empathy and kindness."
> Kevin McCarthy (1980-), First Incarcerated Convict admitted to UC Berkeley

Try applying **THE FORMULA**. What are your Objectives and Options? Do you want to waste and ruin your valuable time by getting depressed or angry — or do you want to figure out a way to achieve better outcomes in the future? How can you act differently next time you face a similar situation — either with that party or in similar situations with other parties? Consider the Results. Can you condition their behavior differently? Can you condition your behavior differently? Be the Master of your Universe.

Once you have assessed the Results of an encounter, feed them into the learning cycle of **The Wisdom Way** to produce more desirable results in the future.

Focus

Focus is important for optimizing group as well as individual performance.

> I once inherited a sales team that was responsible for all the major accounts in the company. My predecessor had reserved every potential large account in the world, which was more than my team could effectively focus upon.
>
> I turned over half of the accounts to the regional sales teams and they were ecstatic. Then I had my team focus on the most promising of the original list.
>
> My team transformed from one of the lowest performing teams in the company to the most successful team once I improved their focus.

Multi-tasking can also be error prone and inefficient. Multi-tasking typically applies to Reflexive Thinking activities where you try to accomplish multiple, simple tasks at the same time. Task-switching applies to more complicated tasks which involve Engaged Thinking.

Switching too frequently can minimize the focus required to accomplish each task effectively. It is also distracting to others involved in a group endeavor.

    According to Elon Musk's biographer, Walter Isaacson, Elon Musk held multiple meetings on the day he first agreed to pay $44 billion for Twitter. Elon met with Indonesia's minister for investment at the Tesla Gigafactory in Austin to discuss battery supply chain, and later on met with engineers at the SpaceX Starbase in Boca Chica, Texas for an hour to discuss valve leak solutions for rocket engines. He reportedly never once mentioned Twitter during those meetings.
    Elon sometimes allocates a whole day at a time to solely focus to each company he owns.

To effectively focus on a single effort, you should shut off all distracting thoughts and interruptions during the timeframe allocated for addressing a complex task. Then you can change your focus to other tasks when you have enough allocated time to make progress on the other tasks.

The Power of Persuasion

    I was at a seminar where the presenter asked an audience of senior business leaders if they would rather increase their intelligence by fifty percent or increase their powers of persuasion by twenty percent.
    Almost everyone in the room chose increasing their powers of persuasion by twenty percent.

The good news is that you do not have to trade off one for the other. The beginning of this book focused on how to master concepts like thinking, learning and memory skills. This section provided concepts and techniques such as establishing rapport, probing, listening and communications

III. MASTERING OTHER UNIVERSES

to help you improve your powers of persuasion and influence with other people.

Try to make sure that you are the one making conscious decisions about who is influencing whom. Other people and entities may be trying to manipulate your Universe with propaganda, marketing, or one-to-one manipulations. Our brains are programmed as primates to find safety in communities with a strong drive to belong to fulfill social needs as well. Be proactive to employ your Engaged Thinking processes to consider your Objectives, Options and the potential Results of your Actions and reactions with other entities — use **THE FORMULA (OO + RRR + AA)**.

**If you want to Master the Universe —
follow The Wisdom Way**

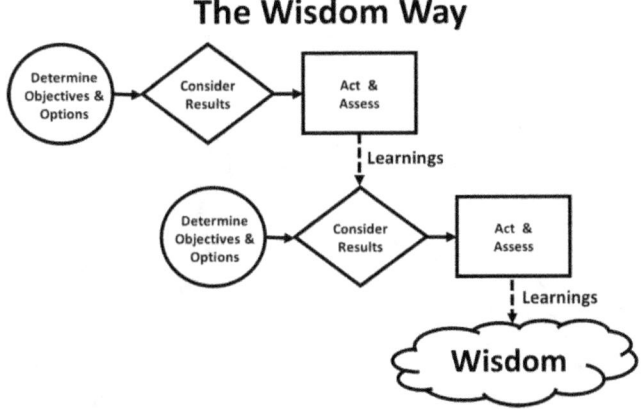

Mastering the Universe is a journey and not a destination. Destinations are endpoints — and endpoints have no future.

Embrace the destinations — and then move on to enjoy the journey.

How To MASTER THE UNIVERSE
Personal and Professional Life-Skills Guide

IV. THE COSMOS

The Cosmos is the Master of itself — and is also driven to survive and thrive under the **COTU Principle**.

"Because our mind is finite, we normally think of the divine perfections separately and hence may not immediately notice the necessity of their being joined together."
Rene Descartes' Ontological Argument

Although we are the centers of our respective Universes, each of us is an infinitesimally small part of The Cosmos. Whenever we try to interrupt the course of The Cosmos, The Cosmos will always work towards righting itself onto its natural path.
.

Cosmos: a complete, orderly, harmonious system.
Dictionary.com

I am using the definition of the Cosmos as the overarching Universe, which is the sum of everything that exists — physical and non-physical. It includes your Universe, my Universe, our souls and bodies, thoughts, animals, and plants — along with other planets, solar systems, galaxies. In the physical world we are living in, it also includes inanimate entities such as mountains, rivers, and rocks. It includes everything that exists and is basically the Universe of Universes.

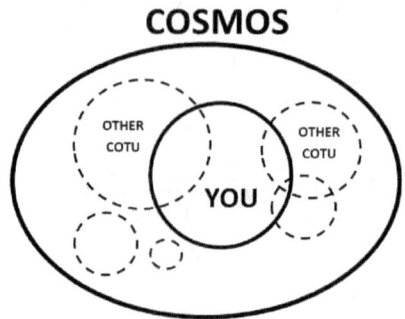

The Cosmos has a consciousness too. Just as we are aware of other entities, other entities have an awareness of events — and an awareness of each other. We can observe awareness between animate entities such as animals by their reactions to other entities. Even though we may not be able to directly perceive awareness in inanimate parts of The Cosmos, they are able to react to other entities and systems as well. Some scientists even attribute consciousness to micro-scale quantum physics events that do not conform to traditional physics.

> **Consciousness:** the state of being conscious; awareness of one's own existence, sensations, thoughts, surroundings, etc.
> *Dictionary.com*

In Integrated Information Theory, consciousness is everywhere, and it accumulates where it is needed to bond with related systems. Our bodies alone have countless interrelated systems within themselves. We interrelate with countless other external entities, which in turn interrelate with an infinite number of systems in The Cosmos.

> "If there is an isolated pair of particles floating around somewhere in space, they will have some rudimentary form of consciousness if they interact in the correct way."
> Johannes Kleiner, Mathematician and Theoretical Physicist

IV. THE COSMOS

Cosmic Balance

"Realize that everything connects to everything else."
Leonardo da Vinci (1452-1519), Artist, Scientist and Architect

Mastering the Universe is a continuous work in progress. Fortunately, we are constantly confronted with new situations or variations of old situations. The differences may be based on different combinations of entities, where each entity has also evolved over time. The same person may react differently tomorrow than they did today based on circumstances they have encountered in between, or they may have had an evolution in their own development. The timing and sequencing may have changed as well. This is fortunate, because it could be extremely boring to evolve to a stage where everything stays the same.

"You must not lose faith in humanity. Humanity is an ocean, if a few drops of the ocean are dirty, the ocean does not become dirty."
Mahatma Gandhi (1869-1948), Indian Civil Rights Leader

If the Cosmos is the total of everything, we are ultimately all connected, directly or indirectly to each other. Intuition can come through us from the rest of the Cosmos and Mindful Thinking can help open the connection. In the section on Thinking I mentioned the concept of the Extended Mind that extends, in the physical world, past the brain into other parts of your body — and even the world around you. We can also open our minds to our soul's physical and social connections to other people and entities. If we are open to this connection and thought flow from the Cosmos, the rest of the Cosmos can create insights, or intuitions which pass through our minds.

> "If you think you are too small to make a difference, try sleeping with a mosquito."
> Dalai Lama IV (1940-), Buddhist Spiritual
> Leader

Meditation and other mindfulness practices can put our brains into an alpha state which opens our intuitive channel. Be aware that intuition can be misleading though, so it helps to run your intuitions through **THE FORMULA** to assess their potential validity.

> "Ty Webb: I'm going to give you a little advice. There's a force in the universe that makes things happen. And all you have to do is get in touch with it, stop thinking, let things happen, and be the ball.
> Ty Webb: Just be the ball, be the ball, be the ball. You're not being the ball, Danny.
> Danny Noonan: It's hard when you're talking like that."
> Caddyshack (1980), Sports Comedy Film

We are not on earth to fix The Cosmos. In the end, the Cosmos will balance itself with or without our interference. What we can do is to control how we react to situations, learn, and make changes that impact our slices of The Cosmos.

> "If you want to change the world, start with yourself."
> Mahatma Gandhi (1869-1948), Indian Civil
> Rights Leader

V. MASTERING OUTCOMES

Succeed: 1. to happen or terminate according to desire; turn out successfully; have the desired result: 2. to thrive, prosper, grow, or the like: 3. to accomplish what is attempted or intended:
Dictionary.com

Succeeding in life is an ongoing process. Even when you succeed with one objective, you will continue to have the opportunity to pursue new objectives.

Life

You will not die — but your body will!

"It's a disgrace in this life when the soul surrenders first while the body refuses to."
Marcus Aurelius (121180 AD), Roman Emperor

"You don't get to choose how you're going to die. Or when. You can only decide how you're going to live. Now."
Joan Baez (1941-), Musician and Activist

All of our bodies are all going to die. It is just a question of when. Organic bodies have a natural life cycle of birth, growing, regenerating, developing, and eventually dying — from natural or unnatural causes. Many of the Individual cells in our bodies die and are replaced by new cells in seven-year cycles and it is possible to rewire your neural networks. There are also scientific efforts to extend life through the introduction of artificial components to our bodies. The artificial components will eventually wear out and the biological components of our bodies will eventually die.

Your soul is hitching a ride in your body — a ride through life. Embrace the moment and enjoy the ride!

When our bodies die, we can live on in one or more manners. Each of us makes a unique impact on the world and other beings with whom we have interacted. We impact their Universes as well as ours. There are even far-reaching ripple effects of how our interactions with one entity affect their interactions with other entities. Our footprint on the world will live on long after our bodies die.

> **Stephen Colbert**: "What do you think happens when we die, Keanu Reeves?"
> **Keanu Reeves:** "I know that the ones who love us will miss us."
> *The Late Show*, May 19, 2021

Our souls may also live on in the spiritual world that extends beyond the physical world. If we're fortunate, we may even have the opportunity to hitch a ride in a future body to experience the joys and struggles of the physical world. If we do, we might reap the good and bad consequences of our earlier actions.

> "That which does not kill us, makes us stronger."
> Friedrich Nietzsche (1844 – 1900), Philosopher

> "And in the end, it's not the years of your life that count. It's the life in your years."
> Abraham Lincoln (1809 – 1865) U. S. President

Reincarnation

Reincarnation is the belief that after a body has died, the

soul has the ability to transmigrate back into the physical world in another body or form. Reincarnation literally means to enter flesh again. The theory of reincarnation — along with Karma — is attractive because it helps rationalize why some people are more fortunate or gifted than others. Or it could explain why one person appears to have worse luck than other people. It offers a motivation to add value during our worldly experience and the penalty of retribution for any negative impact we may have caused. With reincarnation, we can improve our situations and talents across multiple physical lives.

If our souls are the true Center of our Universe and live beyond the physical lifetime of our bodies, it is possible that our souls might have enjoyed multiple ventures into the physical world via past bodies — and more bodily ventures in the future. Even if you do not subscribe to this theory, the practices and applications in the book will help you achieve a more satisfying life.

The belief in reincarnation can be traced in the roots of many early cultures around the world as disconnected as the early North Americans, the ancient Egyptians, Greeks, the Vendas in Southern Africa, and Australian Aboriginal natives. Eastern religions such as Buddhism and Hinduism believe in reincarnation as well as some sub-groups within Christianity, Judaism, and Islam. Several early authors of the Christian Catholic dogma such as Origen of Alexandra were said to believe in reincarnation, but there was debate regarding the viability of variations in potential forms of reincarnation. For example, an early Pope dismissed reincarnation as heretical to believe that a virgin could be reincarnated as a prostitute, or that a man could come back as an animal.

Origen rejected false doctrines of transmigration of souls into other creatures and it is not clear as to what he considered to be true or false interpretations of reincarnation. He did believe in the pre-existence of souls before the creation of the material world and referred to these souls as spiritual intelligences.

When I taught at a Jesuit High School, I used to eat lunch at the rectory instead of the school cafeteria for a couple of reasons. One was that the Jesuits had a gourmet chef in their rectory, and more importantly, I had some great discussions with the Jesuit Priests. Several of the Jesuits had multiple Ph.D.'s. One Priest that I often enjoyed lunch with taught Buddhism at the Loyola College in New Orleans. He told me that he was a practicing Buddhist and a practicing Catholic Priest — and there was no conflict. He said that Buddhism can be more of a philosophy on how to live life than a commitment to a specific organized religion.

Many religions believe that we have a soul, which is offered a chance to experience the physical world by incarnating a body through its lifecycle, and why would this need to be limited to a one-time experience?

Catholicism has a concept called Purgatory. There are debates as to the details regarding Purgatory, but basically, it is a place where a soul goes to atone for its sins if it has not achieved enough perfection to enter heaven. This would be a good description for the act of reincarnation where a soul can reincarnate into a new body to progress or regress in its journey towards a non-physical state. There are parallels to the Hindu concepts around achieving Nirvana. There are benefits to experiencing a physical connection to the world along with potential challenges. In fact, some of our souls may not be in a rush to achieve a non-physical Nirvana and want to enjoy the physical world's benefits as long and often as possible.

I cannot guarantee that reincarnation will occur — but why not stack the deck in your favor.

V. MASTERING OUTCOMES

Virtue

"In spite of everything I still believe that people are really good at heart."
Anne Frank (1929 – 1945), Author and Jewish Holocaust Victim

Good: 1. morally excellent; virtuous; righteous; pious. 2. satisfactory in quality, quantity, or degree. 3. of high quality; excellent.
Bad: 1. not good in any manner or degree. 2. having a wicked or evil character; morally reprehensible. 3. of poor or inferior quality; defective; deficient.
Dictionary.com

Who really wants to be morally reprehensible? Who wants to be of poor or inferior quality; defective; or deficient? Sometimes people's behaviors have been conditioned to behave badly based on anticipated reactions. Maybe there are some people who do not care or are willing to trade off goodness as a shortcut towards satisfying their needs or ambitions. Sometimes they can get away with it during their current lifetime — but lying and cheating to achieve your results is an admission of inferiority. It makes a statement that you are unable or unwilling to perform on comparable terms as others.

"You reap what you sow."
Proverb

Anyone can become better. Anyone can strive for higher quality and excellence. **THE FORMULA** applied to **The Wisdom Way** provides a process for improving and moving towards greatness.

"Don't be afraid to give up the good to go for the great."
John D. Rockefeller (1839-1937), Businessman

Integrity is an important component of virtue. It is a broader concept than honesty alone. Honesty involves telling the truth, sincerity, and the absence of deceit. Integrity includes honesty as well as consistency and completeness. For instance, structural integrity implies that the structure has been constructed to include all the necessary components and is capable of performing its intended function.

>**Integrity:** 1. Adherence to moral and ethical principles; soundness of moral character; honesty. 2. The state of being whole, entire, or undiminished.
>*Dictionary*.com

>"Integrity is doing the right thing even when no one is watching."
>C.S. Lewis (1898-1963), Author

Good virtues can help you achieve the higher levels of Maslow's Pyramid such as Self-Esteem and Self-Actualization. They feed your Karma Pool and might even carry over into future physical lives.

>"Humor and honesty have always been the catalyst for my spiritual growth. When you are so self-serious about the spiritual path, there is no room to grow."
>Baba Ram Dass (1931 – 2019), Author and Harvard Professor

>"Live a good and honorable life. Then, when you are older, you can look back and enjoy it a second time."
>Dalai Lama IV (1940-), Buddhist Spiritual Leader

V. MASTERING OUTCOMES

Attitude

> "Two men looked out prison bars, one saw dirt and the other saw stars."
> Parable

Having a positive attitude is a way to shift the odds of success in your favor. A positive or negative attitude can make the difference between success or failure, so make sure that your attitude is "your" attitude — and not a reflection of someone else's attitude. Own it and do not let others poison your attitude.

Attitudes are contagious and people typically feel better around positive people and enjoy spending time with them. This is one of the reasons why smiling is so contagious. Negative attitudes should be resisted because they are often landmines that can be more contagious than positive attitudes. You may not be able to control every situation, but you can always have control over how you react to the situation.

> "Choose to be optimistic, it feels better."
> "Optimism leads to success; pessimism leads to defeat."
> Dalai Lama IV (1940-), Buddhist Spiritual Leader

You can turn negative events into learning opportunities to facilitate a more successful and happy life. You can condition another party's behaviors to improve future outcomes. And you have control over how you react to situations.

> "There were twin boys who had completely opposite attitudes in life. One was a total pessimist, and the other was a consummate optimist. Their parents were concerned that either extreme could

spell out trouble in life, so on their next birthday the parents came up with a plan to teach each of them a life's lesson.

When the boys woke up on their birthday morning, they took the pessimist to a room full of every toy the boy had ever wanted. The pessimist dejectedly told them that this was the worst day of his life — that he had nothing to look forward to now that he had everything that he had ever desired.

Having failed with the pessimist, the parents hoped for better results with their optimist son. They took him to a room full of horse manure — and he said that it was the best day of his life as he excitedly started digging into the manure. His parents told him that they did not understand his reaction. He said that with all or this horse manure, there must be a pony in there somewhere."

Parable

In this parable the optimist chose to see the positive potential of his situation and considered himself lucky. There are many quotes and examples of the benefits of a positive attitude, but it is worth applying **THE FORMULA** to consider your objectives and possible reactions to your attitude.

"It's hard to beat a person who never gives up."
Babe Ruth (1895-1948), Baseball Player

Simply wishing or visualizing positive outcomes can work against you if you do not also think about your desired outcomes along with the steps and processes required to achieve the positive outcome. For example, simply visualizing a positive outcome on an exam could distract you from taking the actions required to improve your odds of success if you do not also determine and follow through on the studies required to learn the content required to pass the exam.

V. MASTERING OUTCOMES

> "I am a great believer in luck, and I find the harder I work, the more I have of it."
> Thomas Jefferson (1743-1826), Founding Father and U.S. President

If your objective is to establish rapport and influence the behavior of others, you can begin by initially adopting a compatible attitude and pace of others and then lead them by adjusting towards more desirable attitudes — like the example of meshing gears before trying to move them at a different speed and direction.

> "We shouldn't do things so we can be happy, We should be happy so we can do things."
> *The Code of the Extraordinary Mind*, by Vishen Lakhiani

Even though a positive attitude is usually a winning strategy, there are some situations where it is better to adjust to a more appropriate attitude depending on potential reactions in a given situation. For instance, it is typically insensitive to appear too cheery at a funeral. There may be exceptions though, such as when attending a traditional New Orleans funeral. These ceremonies typically start out with walking alongside the casket while singing a mournful song such as "Just A Closer Walk with Thee" to express the sorrow of the loss of the person in this life. Then the ceremony switches to a joyful celebration with a song such as "When the Saints Go Marching In." to commemorate the life the person lived and the hope that the person's soul has transitioned to a better place. This is also an example of meshing and transitioning with the ceremony.

In the book *The Survivors Club*, Ben Sherwood talks about the importance of attitude in critical survival situations. Ben related the belief by legendary survival skills expert, Tom Lutyens, that "80 percent of your survival depends on your attitude; 10 percent on what you know and how you apply it; and 10 percent on the tools and equipment you've got to deal with your challenge."

"The best survival kit is between your ears."
Tom Lutyens, U. S. Airforce Survival Skills Instructor

Rules

The fact is that there are rules in life — and rules can be a good thing or a bad thing for you.

There is often safety in following established rules, but there can be risks as well. Some of the rules that have evolved over centuries based on best practices are very beneficial, but some may have become obsolete, and others may have been established to support another entity's agenda — which may or may not be compatible with your agenda. Some rules are specific to certain cultures and religions and others, like physics apply to meshing with the mechanics of The Cosmos. If you want to **Master the Universe**, you should be open to questioning the rules.

Rules can be influenced by Absolute Truths or Relative Truths, including assumptions, or opinions. Absolute Truths are ones that exist without the influence or interpretations of other entities. Gravity on our planet follows the rules of an Absolute Truth. If you drop exactly similar objects under the same conditions, they will fall at the same rate of speed. Rules based on Absolute Truths can be questioned and sometimes improved based on the incorporation of updated and more relevant data.

Farmers successfully produced food by following accepted rules and methods for farming in the 19th century based on what were considered Absolute Truths at the time, some of which became obsolete. Since then, advancements in technology and science have enabled farmers to significantly improve their production by applying new rules based on an improved set of truths. New information can be used to update truths that were previously considered as Absolute Truths.

V. MASTERING OUTCOMES

> "A mind is like a parachute. It doesn't work if it isn't open."
> Frank Zappa (1940-1993), Musician

Rules that are influenced by Relative Truths such as the ones coming from society, religions and other entities can be valuable as well. Rules establish behavioral protocols that make it easier to interact with others and the community at large. Some religious rules supported safety and healthier lifestyles when the rules were created based on the best information available at the time. Eating poorly cooked pork proved to be dangerous and some religions established rules against eating pork. Taking a day of rest every week has been shown to be a healthy practice which became a rule in some religions. Be wary of rules based upon Relative Truths because they may have been formed for ulterior purposes or based upon obsolete or flawed information and opinions.

> "If you can't win, change the rules. If you can't change the rules, ignore them."
> Peter Diamandis (1961-), Co-Founder of
> Singularity University

You do not have to be locked into pre-existing rules. Following established rules is analogous to Reflexive Thinking where you do not have to expend unnecessary energy and time to interoperate with others. In some cases, changing the rules or playing by different rules can be very advantageous — and is not cheating unless you have agreed to play by conflicting rules.

> I was once in a management training seminar where one of the first exercises was about "thinking outside the box," which is a form of thinking outside of established rules.
> During the next exercise, the instructor separated us into small teams, each with a set of materials including an egg, popsicle sticks, tape, and rubber bands. The instructions were for the team to take 10 minutes to plan a structure and then

5 minutes to build a structure to keep the egg from breaking when dropped from a height of six feet. When we started our group's planning session, I noticed that there was a coffee pot in the back of the room and suggested that we apply our "thinking outside the box" lesson and hard boil the egg in the coffee pot during our planning session — and then build the structure around it.

When it came to the final test, our egg did not break. We had applied the previous lesson and played by different rules than the other teams — to win the challenge.

It takes extra effort to utilize Engaged Thinking to challenge a rule. If you question the value of an established rule, you can employ **THE FORMULA (OO + RRR + AA)** to assess the value of changing or continuing to follow a rule. Think about your objectives and options. Think about the potential Rewards, Reactions or Results that will impact you and others. Then if you chose to Act, Assess the results to determine your willingness to follow, change or ignore established rules in the future.

Self-determination

You have the power to change the course of your Universe.

You can change the course of other Universes too. Just remember that The Cosmos and other Universes are working towards satisfying the **COTU Principle** from their perspectives too.

> "Everyone believes the world's greatest lie..." says the mysterious old man. "What is the world's greatest lie?" the little boy asks. The old man replies, "It's this: that at a certain point in our lives,

V. MASTERING OUTCOMES

we lose control of what's happening to us, and our lives become controlled by fate."
The Alchemist, by Paulo Coelho

It is easier to control your future if you mesh with the power of The Cosmos and other Universes before changing directions as discussed in the Rapport Section. You can make decisions that will change your future, the futures of adjacent Universes and trickle through their chains of influence. It will be easier if you try the Jiu-Jitsu approach described in the Conflicts Section.

"Trends are like horses. They are easier to ride in the direction they are traveling."
Proverb

By definition, the future is not here yet. So, outcomes are not pre-determined — even if there is an omnipotent being that knows your decisions in advance. This still means that you have the capacity for self-determination.

Mistakes

Ground control had a target programmed into Robbie the Rocket before he launched. When Robbie was early in his flight, he checked with the control tower to see if he was still on target. Ground control signaled back that he was a few degrees off to the north and east.
Robbie adjusted his direction and checked back a little later to learn that he needed to make another adjustment. This process continued throughout the flight. In the end, Robbie hit his target.
Did Robbie make mistakes — sure, but he constantly adjusted to small, correctable mistakes rather than wait to analyze his progress until he was too off course to reach his target.
Networking Conference Anecdote by John Cleese (1939-), Comedian, and Author

The Robbie the Rocket story is an example of applying **THE FORMULA (OO + RRR + AA)** through the cycles of **The Wisdom Way** to achieve the mission. Robbie had a set Objective to reach the target. There were multiple Options to adjust his trajectory along the way. He calculated the potential Results from the Options and Acted accordingly to adjust his course. Then he continued Assessing the results of his Actions throughout the mission and fed the information back into the next cycle of applying **THE FORMULA** to his decision process.

> "Every strike brings me closer to the next home run."
> Babe Ruth (1895-1948), Baseball Player

In 2021, *Fortune Magazine* ranked Amazon as the second largest and second most admired company in America. Amazon's founder, Jeff Bezos has often been ranked the richest man in the world. Do Jeff Bezos and Amazon make mistakes? They have made a lot of mistakes. Amazon's history is littered with failed projects, including the Fire Phone, a travel site called Destinations, Amazon Wallet, a mobile card processing site called Amazon Local Register, Music Importer for downloading songs, Test Drive, Amazon Web Pay, Endless.com for high end clothes, and Askville. Making mistakes does not make you a failure but failing to learn from your mistakes will.

> "When you make a mistake, there are only three things you should ever do about it: admit it, learn from it, and do not repeat it."
> Paul "Bear" Bryant (1913 – 1983), American Football Coach

When you do make a mistake, try to "fail fast" and move on as quickly as possible. Admit your mistakes to yourself — and to others when appropriate. We all make mistakes as part of our learning process and other people will admire you all the more if you are mature enough to admit when you have been wrong.

> "If you keep doing what you've always done, you keep on getting what you've always got."
> Hannibal Barca (~247 – 183 BC), Carthaginian General

If you manage it properly, failure can be luck in disguise by helping steer us away from old approaches — until we discover better solutions.

> "Mistakes are the portals of discovery."
> James Joyce (1882–1941), Author

> "I can accept failure. Everyone fails at something. But I can't accept not trying."
> Michael Jordan (1963-), Basketball Star and Businessman

Sometimes you must play the odds on a decision based on the alternatives you are aware of at the time. You can make a good decision that turns out to fail because the result went against the odds, or there were variables you were unaware of at the time, or the dynamics impacting the decision changed. If a decision fails, it does not necessarily mean that you made a bad decision.

> "Success is falling nine times and getting up 10."
> Jon Bon Jovi (1962-) Musician and Actor

Assess whether it is best to decide more quickly, even if there are unknown dynamics involved. You might lose an opportunity entirely by waiting too long and decide that it would be better to take a chance on a mistake that you can learn from.

> "A ship that is fully prepared never leaves port."
> Proverb

"Fortune favors the bold."
"Aeneid" (19 BC), by Virgil, Roman Poet

Apply the Assessing step of **THE FORMULA** to feed into the next cycle of **The Wisdom Way** and do not waste time on guilt. Guilt, like worry, is not constructive. Neither will not change a previous decision or action. They will only slow you down and hamper your attitude. Ask yourself instead what you can learn from the mistake and how can you make better decisions in the future?

"We haven't failed. We know a thousand things that won't work, so we're that much closer to finding what will."
Thomas Edison (1847 – 1931), Inventor

Do not worry about what you have no control over — and get control over whatever might worry you.

You cannot change the past — but you can make the best of the present, and you can change the future.

"I don't believe in having regrets. Things happen and you get what you deserve."
Craig Alexander (1973-), 3 time Ironman Triathlon World Champion

Karma

People call me lucky — but I like to think that it is Karma.
Karma: seen as bringing upon oneself inevitable results, good or bad, either in this life or in a reincarnation.
Luck: the force that seems to operate for good or ill in a person's life, as in shaping circumstances,

V. MASTERING OUTCOMES

events, or opportunities:
Chance: the absence of any cause of events that can be predicted, understood, or controlled: *Dictionary.com*

The operant word in this definition of Luck, is the word "seems." The cause of the force shaping the circumstances could come from Karma or simply the statistical Chance of the situation. You can positively impact your life though Karma. You can increase your Luck by influencing circumstances, events, or opportunities. And you can also improve your Chances by choosing options with better statistical odds.

> "Service to others is the rent you pay for the room you have here on earth."
> Mohammed Ali (1942-2016) Professional Boxer

A basic level of Karma is Transactional Karma where one deed is directly tied to another deed.

A higher level of Karma is achieved by contributing to what I will refer to as the Karma Pool, where you are not expecting a direct payback for your deeds. You are performing good or bad deeds that will be rewarded or punished in the future — sometimes by the same entity and sometimes by others. When you contribute to the Karma Pool, you can think of it as earning Karma Credit that will return value back to you in this life, or possibly in future lives.

> "Carry out a random act of kindness, with no expectation of reward, safe in the knowledge that one day someone might do the same for you."
> Princess Diana (1961-1997), Princess of Wales

You can rationalize a good or bad circumstance to be the consequence of Karma, luck — or simply because of the Chance of being caught in the broader dynamics taking place in the Cosmos.

> "The amount of good luck coming your way depends on your willingness to act."
> Barbara Sher (1935-2020), Author and Career/lifestyle Coach

Sometimes you can have an impact on specific situations — but other times the cause of the circumstances are based on dynamics that are out of your control. What you can always do is control the way you choose to react to the situation. You can decide if you want to make the best of good situations. Or you can decide if you want to turn bad situations into better situations by learning from them by applying **THE FORMULA (OO + RRR + AA)** and then feeding your learnings into **The Wisdom Way** cycle of learning. If you learn and prepare yourself for future situations, you will have a better chance of improving your luck.

> "Luck is preparation meeting opportunity."
> Seneca (54 BC – 39 AD)

> "Fortune favors the prepared mind."
> Louis Pasteur (1822-1895), Chemist and Microbiologist

Bad deeds can detract from your Karma Pool just as good deeds can add Karma Credit to your Karma Pool — and increase the likelihood of better circumstances in the future. This is a form of "Paying it Forward" with Karma Credit.

> "The maintenance laws of golf — replace your divot, repair ball marks on greens — are not just courtesies to golfers who will follow nor simple respect for those who made the course what it is. They function as an antidote to the suffering that golf provides a man in the moment that he sees how good a golfer he is at the same time that he sees how

V. MASTERING OUTCOMES

good a golfer he thinks he is."
Bill Murray (1950-), Actor, Comedian, and Writer

Operant Conditioning is another form of Paying it Forward. Seeding future behaviors helps create Virtuous Cycles of behavior — or Vicious Cycles of behavior.

"10% of life is purely random. The remaining 90% is "actually defined by the way you think."
Richard Wiseman (1966-), Author and Psychology Professor

The Cosmos, being the overarching Universe of Universes, also subscribes to **The COTU Principal** and is driven to survive and thrive. The Karma of The Cosmos can take precedence over your own Karma in specific situations. The Cosmos also must arbitrate the relative fairness and balance to all of the Universes involved.

It is The Cosmos that "imposes order and regularity on aggregates of more or less disparate elements." This is fair for the Cosmos, but it is possible for you to be inadvertently impacted negatively by Chance — even if you were not directly responsible for your outcome. Sometimes the fairness of a situation is simply based on the needs of the Cosmos.

Becoming the best one-to-one combat fighter in an army would increase your statistical odds of survival and success. But there is no guarantee that you might be eliminated by chance, sheer numbers, or by a random bomb landing next to you.

You could also work hard all your life to become healthy and physically fit but could die by chance in an earthquake if you are in the wrong place when the earth needs to adjust its tectonic plates. Whatever the Cosmos needs to do to right itself may be fair in the aggregate but may not seem fair for each recipient from a transactional karma perspective. However, your likelihood of success is improved by playing the odds as best as you can.

Taking a vaccine for a disease is another example of playing the odds. There is a small chance that you could have an adverse reaction to a vaccine, but the risk is often overwhelmingly offset by the odds and benefits of improved protection provided by the vaccine against the impact of the disease.

It is difficult to fight the momentum of the Cosmos trying to right itself. It is easier to take a "Jiu Jitsu" approach — as described in the Conflicts section, than to take a "karate" approach when dealing with the overwhelming momentum of the Cosmos.

> "You don't just luck into things as much as you'd like to think you do. You build step by step, whether it's friendships or opportunities."
> Barbara Bush (1925-2018), 41st First Lady of the United States

Attributes common to lucky people include their positive attitudes — they identify with the positive aspects of situation; they network well with other people — and people help them achieve better outcomes. They position themselves for better outcomes — they are better prepared for situations and play better odds, and they invest in their Karma Pools.

> The Karma Pool is like an expandible pool where you add handfuls of gold dust every time you perform a good deed to earn positive Karma Credit. This is not an exact science where you can measure the exact value of each handful.
> If you perform bad deeds, you take away handfuls of gold dust. And if your bad deeds empty the pool of its gold dust, you start adding handfuls of toxic waste. Fortunately, performing good deeds will take away handfuls of toxic waste until you start adding gold dust back into the pool with your good deeds.
> The gold dust has positive value in life and the toxic waste has negative value.

V. MASTERING OUTCOMES

How do you beat the statistical odds? By investing positive Karma Credit into your Karma Pool. Developing simple habits of performing good deeds is an easy way to add massive amounts of positive Karma Credit to your Karma Pool.

> When I was a young salesperson, I used to keep a slip of paper pinned to my cubicle in front of my eyes. It had an image of two starving buzzards sitting on a tree branch, and one of them was saying to the other, "Patience my ass, I'm going out and kill something."

You should not sit around waiting for good Karma to happen to you. Sometimes you need to go out and find or create opportunities for yourself — as well as pro-actively spreading your good Karma to others.

> "When you truly understand karma, then you realize you are responsible for everything in your life."
> Keanu Reeves (1964-), Actor

Gratitude

You are responsible for your own Universe, so the meaning of life for you is whatever you want it to be.

You are fortunate — even by the fact that you are reading a book right now. Others are less fortunate, whether from the consequences of weak Karma Pools or luck due to random chance. Approximately 13% of the people in the world over 15 years old are illiterate. Over 9% of the people live in extreme poverty, with approximately 25,000 people dying of starvation every day. Hundreds of millions of people are struggling to achieve the Survival level of Maslow's Pyramid — and you are working on satisfying the higher levels of needs.

You are also fortunate to live in a time where there are so many options for health care, food, education, science, travel, entertainment. There are still risks, such as disease, starvation, and war. These factors have been top causes of human death — but have been greatly reduced over recent years. The average person in the world today has a far better lifestyle than the richest and most powerful people on earth one hundred years ago — and at any previous time in history.

> "YOU ARE THE CHOSEN ONE: Do you choose your calling, or does your calling choose you? There is a model of reality emerging that suggests that the universe (Cosmos) comes calling – and your job is to listen."
> *Code of the Extraordinary Mind,* by Vishen Lakhiani

There are reasons why our souls want to hitch a ride in a body, even though physical life includes pain along with pleasure. You can find reasons to be unhappy or reasons to justify happiness. You get to decide what quality of life means to you.

Is your quality of life determined by happiness, knowledge, wisdom, love, respect, progress towards Self-Actualization or something else?

If the Cosmos has a mission and chooses you to manifest that mission, you can seize the opportunity — or else the Cosmos will find another entity willing to help fulfill its destiny. If you listen to your intuition, it may be the Cosmos sending a message through your mind. Over time, the Cosmos learns who will move initiatives forward and proceeds to provide more and more opportunities to those that help fulfill its destiny. This process becomes a form of manifest destiny.

V. MASTERING OUTCOMES

> "To live a good life: We have the potential for it. If we learn to be indifferent to what makes no difference."
>
> "Because most of what we say and do is not essential. Ask yourself at every moment, "Is this necessary?"
>
> Marcus Aurelius (121-180 AD), Roman Emperor

Our souls have limited access to the physical world through our bodies, so we should be grateful and make the best of this opportunity. A good candidate for a meaning of life is to enjoy the opportunity to co-exist in the physical world. To touch, see, breathe, smell, hear, and taste. We can optimize our time by taking care of our bodies, our brains, eyes, ears, tactile sensations, and interactions with other physical entities.

> "Be thankful for what you have; you'll end up having more. If you concentrate on what you don't have, you will never, ever have enough."
>
> Oprah Winfrey (1954-), Talk Show Host and Author

Also, if reincarnation works and you are going to have an opportunity to utilize a future body — why not try to help improve the world for yourself in the future while making it better for others. The next body we latch onto, and the next life we live may be influenced or determined by the contribution we have made to the evolution of the Cosmos during this lifetime.

> "There are only two ways to live your life. One is as though nothing is a miracle. The other is as though everything is a miracle."
>
> Albert Einstein (1879-1955), Theoretical Physicist

Do not forget to show gratitude to others too. Showing gratitude to others makes them feel better. It is a way of reinforcing their desired behaviors. And it helps feed your Karma Pool.

Choices

> "I can't change the direction of the wind, but I can adjust my sails to always reach my destination."
> James Dean (1931-1955), American Actor

The introduction of the book asked, "If you had a choice, would you rather improve your mental abilities — or improve your powers of persuasion?" If you had a choice, would you rather be smarter — or improve your powers of persuasion? Would you rather be right — or would you rather win? Do you want to be good — or to be lucky?" None of these are either/or choices. You can achieve them all and more by choosing to apply **THE FORMULA** to your thinking process — and to your interactions with others.

> "Be the change you wish to see in the world."
> Mahatma Gandhi (1869-1948), Indian Civil Rights Leader

Your ability to **Master the Universe** is under your control. It is directly related to your choices. You can choose joy or choose sorrow by how you react to situations. You can focus on pleasure, or you can let pain overwhelm you. You can choose good habits or bad habits. You can contribute to your Karma Pool with good actions or sabotage it with bad behavior. And you can choose to slow down to contemplate the steps of **THE FORMULA** with Engaged Thinking or you can simply assume that you are making the best decisions through Reactive Thinking. You can learn from your experiences or ignore them.

V. MASTERING OUTCOMES

> "The happiness of your life depends upon the quality of your thoughts."
> Marcus Aurelius (121-180 AD), Roman Emperor

Since the Cosmos is always working towards righting itself, and it is a more powerful force than any subordinate Universe. It is easier to mesh and flow with the Cosmos whenever you can — and use your mind and brain to decide what you want to influence or control. If something seems impossible or not worth the effort to control — stop worrying about it. You can always bookmark and revisit it later. Making it your decision puts it in your control.

> "I am the master of my fate:
> I am the captain of my soul."
> "Invictus" by William Ernest Henley (1849-1903)

> "If you don't like the road you're walking, start paving another one."
> Dolly Parton (1946-), Singer, Songwriter and Actress

Success: Money vs. Karma

> "If you think you're so smart, why aren't you rich?"
> Proverb

Being rich depends on the definitions you choose for the words "rich" and "wealth." It also depends on how you decide to measure success. Success in your business or career should be a subset of your overall success in life. You cannot take monetary success with you when you die, but you can leave a legacy of wealth and good deeds for others. And if you believe in Heaven, Hell, or reincarnation — you can take your Karma Credit along for the ride.

>**Rich:** 1. Having wealth or great possessions, abundantly supplied with resources, means or funds; wealthy.
>**Wealth:** 1. a great quantity or store of money, valuable possessions, property, or other riches. 2. an abundance or profusion of anything.
>*Dictionary.com*

In business and careers, success is often measured in financial terms. Money and wealth are used as success metrics for the value provided to customers, investors, partners, and employees.

Many non-monetary accomplishments can be more important than your monetary measures of success. Success can also be measured by "an abundance or profusion of anything," such as producing results that improve lives, create new opportunities, save the environment, increase safety, create good will, and improve the world in general.

>"Money often costs too much."
>Ralph Waldo Emerson (1803-1882), Author

Fortunately, a business or career can directly contribute to non-monetary accomplishments — and money can be used as an exchange for making these contributions. Other times these contributions can be made without the involvement of your business or career.

>"To live well is to work well — to show a good activity."
>Thomas Aquinas (1225-1274), Philosopher and Theologian

One currency of success is the accumulation of Karma Credit by you or your business. Appropriate monetary or non-monetary contributions can be considered investments in a Karma Pool. Unlike money, Karma Credits are general,

V. MASTERING OUTCOMES

fluid, and intangible assets which are difficult to measure. This is one of the reasons for using the term "pool" instead of calling it an "exchange."

Success in business, or life in general, is rated on different scales than it is in school. In school, you are typically rated on a 0-100 scale. In life, you can produce negative results — or excel past 100%. In business you can drop below a 0% return on a business transaction and lose money — your money and other people's money — or you can make a healthy profit beyond 100%. In life you can make an unlimited number of positive contributions to the world.

We all need to satisfy the lower levels of Maslow's Hierarchy of Needs Pyramid to survive in the physical world. This includes the need for eating, drinking, breathing, and sleeping. We also need to satisfy the next level of Safety Needs, which includes shelter and healthcare for a longer life. Money provides an exchange medium for the indirect work or value that we add to the world to help satisfy these basic needs. Money also provides a mechanism to save and be prepared for future Physiological and Safety Needs.

> **COTU Principle:** Every entity is the Center of its own Universe and is motivated by its own survival and success.

It is important to work hard to earn enough to satisfy these basic Physiological and Safety Needs — which are survival needs. These needs can be satisfied through activities such as living off the land, but they are more easily satisfied using money as an exchange medium.

As you move up Maslow's Hierarchy of Needs into Social Needs, monetary exchanges can help, but non-monetary exchange mediums such as positive actions and Karma Credit can supersede the value of monetary transactions. The need for money becomes more of a question as to how much you're willing to put into the equation and its effect on your outcome.

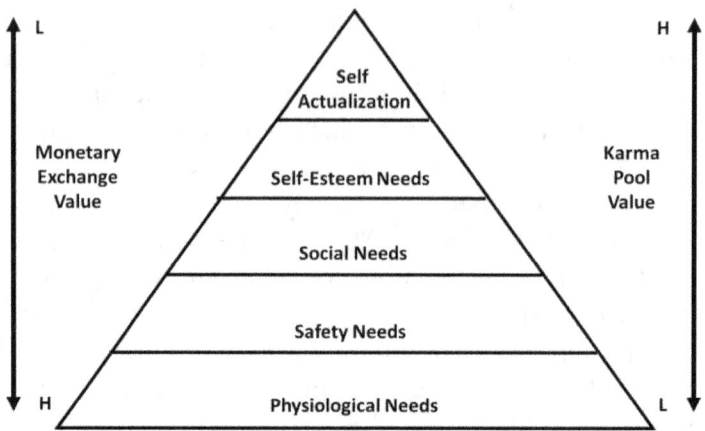

It is easier to satisfy Self-Esteem Needs without money than it is to satisfy your basic Needs without money. Money can help as an exchange medium, but you can also achieve Self-Esteem via good deeds, and personal accomplishments.

Self-Actualization: the achievement of one's full potential through creativity, independence, spontaneity, and a grasp of the real world.
Dictionary.com

Achieving Self-Actualization has little-to-nothing to do with financial exchanges. You need to satisfy your basic needs and beyond that, there are many things that you can do without monetary exchanges that are more valuable than what you may have to sacrifice to earn more money.

Monetary donations to worthy causes may help satisfy Social and Esteem Needs — but they will only aid Self Actualization if the cost of acquiring the money does not create more damage that the benefits it provides.

A satisfying career can also help satisfy Self

V. MASTERING OUTCOMES

Actualization Needs. You can add value to Self-Actualization through your profession, career or through volunteer work to help individuals or the community. Ideally you can find a professional career that contributes to the betterment of the world and Cosmos and adds value to your Karma Pool too.

> "You can't always get what you want . . ."
> ". . . You get what you need,"
> Keith Richards & Mick Jagger (1943-) Rolling Stones Band

Think about what is "enough" for you to survive and achieve success. Do you have enough to live a safe and satisfying life? What is the inflection point where you have earned "enough?" What do you have to do in exchange for survival and success in life? What are the trade-offs? Do the costs exceed the benefits?

> "You never know what is enough unless you know what is more than enough."
> *The Marriage of Heaven and Hell* by William Blake (1757-1827)

Are you sacrificing too many hours away from your family to earn more than enough? Are you creating too much anxiety which is affecting your health or other undesirable trade-offs to earn more? It is fine to earn "more than enough" if you are not sacrificing more than you are earning. It is even better to earn more than "enough" if you enjoy your vocation.

> Research has shown that beyond a moderate salary level, people typically do not experience an increased satisfaction level. In the long run, happiness is more dependent on your balance in life, the quality of your relationships and your career satisfaction.

Establishing healthy micro-habits for happiness can be more satisfying than constantly chasing new financial goals. Whenever you achieve a milestone, take time to celebrate this success before moving on to your next set of objectives. If you keep making "enough" a moving target, without celebrating, you will never be satisfied. Do not move the goalpost for the sake of social comparison — move it to accomplish your own definitions of success.

Do not confuse Self-Esteem with Other-Esteem.

You can always find someone with more wealth or higher earnings than you, but you are in charge if deciding what you need to achieve a balance of security and happiness.

> "Earth provides enough to satisfy every man's needs, but not every man's greed."
> Mahatma Gandhi (1869-1948), Indian Civil Rights Leader

If you decide that earning "enough" is $50,000 per year in earnings and $200,000 in savings, then it is fine to keep earning and saving more if it contributes to a more rewarding life.

It is worthwhile to step back and think through **THE FORMULA (OO + RRR + AA)**. What are your Objectives? What are the potential outcomes? Are you earning enough to satisfy you and your family's basic survival needs? What are the monetary or non-monetary rewards of the options?

> "For what shall it profit a man, if he should gain the whole world, and suffer the loss of his soul?"
> Jesus Christ (4BC-30 or 33AD), Religious Leader and Teacher

If you get to the point where, within reason, you can do anything you want, whenever you want, with whomever you want — money no longer becomes the priority.

V. MASTERING OUTCOMES

> "Those who want the fewest things are nearest to the gods."
> Socrates (470BC-399BC) Greek Philosopher

Next

> "Time is the most valuable thing that a man can spend."
> Diogenes (412-323 BC), Philosopher

We have discussed a lot of concepts and practices in this book to better master your personal Universe and the other Universes that exist. The concepts and practices are primarily based on the **COTU Principle** that you are the Center of the Universe — just as everyone else is The Center of their Universe.

> "When you're finished changing, you're finished."
> Benjamin Franklin (1706–1790), United States Founding Father

There is a difference between teaching and training. I have discussed concepts, which is a form of teaching, but you really need training to embed new behaviors. For a practice to become a habitual behavior requires repetition. That is one of the reasons that it is called "a practice." You can train yourself or you can seek out guidance from other sources. For more effective training, you should seek feedback too. Take more in-depth training courses on the topics that I have reviewed and seek out some good mentors. Sometimes you may forget to apply the steps to **THE FORMULA (OO + RRR + AA)**, but the more you practice it, the more it will become a natural part of your behavior. It is valuable to keep learning and make continuous improvements throughout the different phases of our lives.

"The best time to plant a tree was 20 years ago. The second-best time is now."
Chinese proverb

Adult Learning Phases*:

1. Early Adulthood (15-25) – Take the right risks.
2. Emerging Adulthood (25-45) – Absorb and reflect.
3. Established Adulthood (45-60) – Do not get too big to fail.
4. Late Adulthood (60+) – Prune and Graft.
   *Based on research by Boris Groysberg and Robin Abrahams

Satisfying physical needs such as sleep, exercise, meditation, and nutrition help facilitate more effective learning, memory, judgement, moods, and insights throughout the Adult Learning Phases. Your environment also plays an important role throughout the process, with different emphasis in the various phases.

Early Adults (15-25) are at the peak of their memory and information processing capabilities, but their wisdom is limited by their lack of experience. They are typically driven to seek novelty and take risks. Their driving environmental concern is with the opinion of their peers. They need to take risks to gain experience and develop good habits. And should try to avoid compromising their learning opportunities due to fear of failing in front of their peers.

Emerging Adults (25-45) are in an exciting period where they have the benefits of physically mature brains, youthful immune systems and early wisdom gained from real-world experiences. They also have experienced a variety of environmental, social, and professional roles such as student, occupation, spouse, parent, team/organizational membership, and hobbies. To optimize learning in this phase, they should create the time and space to absorb and reflect on the lessons gained across their various experiences. This is a good time to integrate the cross-learnings from their experiences, develop cross-generational relationships — and to create and reinforce constructive habits.

Members of the Established Adulthood (45-60) phase should avoid becoming too big to fail. Memory and analytic skills start to slow down but this can be offset by leveraging the learnings from decades of experience, relationship networks, self-awareness, and positive habits. This is a good period to continue to take calculated risks to expand your comfort zone, while keeping open to continued learning.

In Established Adulthood (60+) people tend to prune and graft. Even though life human lifecycles are expanding, physiological capabilities such as memory, attention, and analytical skills start to decline. Established Adults are less driven by novelty and can resist new experiences. They start "pruning" by reducing and prioritizing their range of interests. And then "grafting" by combining these interests when possible and being open to adding new interests. They can make the best of this phase by the multiplicative effect of combining physical activities, to maintain physical capabilities, while engaging their minds in activities to maintain their thinking skills.

To fully enjoy the opportunity to experience each phase of life, it is important to tend to your physical needs and to continue developing your learning skills. The concepts in this book are intended to spark your interest in developing these skills and to become starting points for the rest of your journey.

> "The most excellent jihad is the conquest of one's self."
> Muhammad (~570-632), Religious Leader

The first sentence of this book is "You are the **Center of the Universe!**" Accordingly, this book has been focused on you and techniques for you to interact more effectively with others. If you work on continually improving yourself, treating others as if they are the **Center of the Universe**, and apply **THE FORMULA,** you will be able to experience a more fulfilling life.

> "Do not serve time, let time serve you."
> Willie Sutton, (1901-1980), American Bank Robber

Don't just apply **THE FORMULA** to specific situations — apply it to life in general. Follow **The Wisdom Way**. Set check points where you will take the time to think through your objectives and the results your current habits are producing. Like Robbie the Robot, think about how you are going to adjust your habits to re-adjust your life's course. Set big visions and break them down into achievable milestones — and periodically reassess your progress.

> "You have power over your mind — not outside events. Realize this, and you will find strength."
> Marcus Aurelius (121-180 AD), Roman Emperor

COTU Principle: Every entity is the Center of its own Universe and is motivated by its own survival and success.

> "Enjoy life. There is plenty of time to be dead."
> Hans Christian Anderson (1805-1875), Danish Author

One Purpose of Life is to make the best of your time in the world — the time in your body. To do so, determine your objectives, then follow through with the rest of **THE FORMULA** and refine the process via **The Wisdom Way**.

> "Every day, think as you wake up: Today I am fortunate to be alive, I have a precious human life, I am not going to waste it."
> Dalai Lama IV (1940-), Buddhist Spiritual Leader

V. MASTERING OUTCOMES

Master The Universe Formula
THE FORMULA = OO + RRR + AA

1. **OO** – Determine your Objectives and Options.
2. **RRR** – Consider potential Results, Reactions, and Rewards to determine your course of action.
3. **AA** – Act and Assess.

PRO TIP: Use the condensed acronym **"ORA"** to remember **THE FORMULA.**

**If you want to Master the Universe —
follow The Wisdom Way**

The Wisdom Way

Mastering the Universe is a journey and not a destination. Destinations are endpoints — and endpoints have no future.

Embrace the destinations — and then move on to enjoy the journey.

How To MASTER THE UNIVERSE
Personal and Professional Life-Skills Guide

ADDENDUM: BUSINESS & PROFESSIONAL SKILLS

> Do what you love,
> And love what you do.
> Seek pride and perfection,
> And you will master your profession.

Mastering your profession can play a key role in mastering the Universe. People often invest a significant amount of their waking hours towards their profession or their business. Mastering it can help improve your life as well as the lives of others.

> **Business:** 1. an occupation, profession, or trade; 2. the purchase and sale of goods in an attempt to make a profit.
> *Dictionary.com*

This Section is applicable towards occupations in general and the utility of money as an exchange medium. The first definition of business does not require the exchange of goods in an attempt to make a profit. Many of the principles covered in this section can be applied to a non-profit organization or career.

I will review some of the general concepts of business and provide some practical examples of how to apply the **COTU Principle** (Center of the Universe Principle) and the Mastering the Universe FORMULA in a business environment.

> **COTU Principle:** Every entity is the Center of its own Universe and is motivated by its own survival and success.

I will start out by establishing a baseline for the terms business, money, profits, and capitalism — and then discuss some practical applications. The examples are in not meant to be all-inclusive. Instead, they are intended to spark your interest in exploring other ways to leverage **THE FORMULA** in a business environment.

Master The Universe Formula
THE FORMULA = OO + RRR + AA

1. **OO** – Determine your Objectives and Options.
2. **RRR** – Consider potential Results, Reactions, and Rewards to determine your course of action.
3. **AA** – Act and Assess.

PRO TIP: Use the condensed acronym **"ORA"** to remember **THE FORMULA.**

Money & Profit

"Don't go around saying the world owes you a living. The world owes you nothing. It was here first."
Mark Twain (1835–1910) American author

Given a choice, would you want more money or a better life? I will discuss the concept of money in this section. In the earlier section on Success, we discussed how it might apply to your success in life.

Business typically involves the act of exchanging objects or services of value for other objects or services of value. Profits occur when the exchange creates increased value for either, or ideally, both parties.

"Business, that's easily defined. It's other people's money."
Peter Drucker (1909–2005), Management Consultant

Business transactions can occur though barter with the direct exchange of goods or services; or they can occur via a symbolic exchange medium like money. Using a symbolic exchange medium became more efficient than barter because one of the parties involved in the exchange does not always have something of direct exchange value to the other party's Universe. The use of money enables the opportunity to profit from multi-party transactions. For example, the purchase of a good or service from one party and profiting by adding some additional value and reselling the good or service to another party at a higher price.

Money started out as a symbolic exchange medium with its own inherent material value — for example, the weight of a gold coin. Money later evolved into representing virtual value — for example, paper currency backed by trusted entities like governments. Monetary transactions even became virtual by exchanging account balances instead of actually transferring physical currencies. The latest evolution of virtual currencies includes cryptocurrencies like Bitcoin, which relies upon unique mathematical algorithms and chains of dispersed transaction ledgers called Blockchains for unique validation of its value.

Money is not inherently good or evil. It is simply an exchange medium for value between two or more party's Universes. In fact, I once read about a religious minister who preached about the virtues of money and profits. He preached that you could set a good example for others by honestly profiting as much as possible, even for a religious preacher to profit from his or her own ministry.

> Money can be good or evil — depending on how you earn it and how you spend it.

Religious organizations are usually happy to receive money as an exchange medium for the value they provide. After all, honest money is one measurement of having provided value to other parties. It is also an efficient exchange medium to provide for your own basic needs and for the initiatives and people you want to support.

An example of the power of the exchange value of money is the placebo effect on the cost of a drug or treatment. Studies have shown that placebos (fake drugs or treatments) can sometimes work as effectively as the actual drugs. Researchers discovered that the more they charged for a drug or placebo, the more effective were the results perceived by the patients. In other words, the symbolic value of the exchange affected the perceived value.

> "What surprises me most is "Man" because he sacrifices his health in order to make money. Then he sacrifices money to recuperate his health. And then he is so anxious about the future that he doesn't enjoy the present; The result being he doesn't live in the present or the future; He lives as if he's never going to die, and then he dies having never really lived."
> Dalai Lama IV (1940-), Buddhist Spiritual Leader

So back to the original question at the beginning of this section; would you want more money or a better life — a better life for you and/or others? If you want a better life, and money is just an exchange medium, only pursue more money when the cost of the money is worth the additional benefits it affords you. For example, if you need to sacrifice your health, longevity, values, enjoyment and/or relationships that you value to acquire more money — question if the sacrifice is worth the cost. On the other hand, if you can honestly add more value to others in exchange for more money, and the money can improve your health, longevity, values, enjoyment and/or relationships, then it's a worth the effort.

> "I didn't get there by wishing for it or hoping for it, but by working for it."
> Estée Lauder (1906-2004), Businesswoman

Honest Capitalism

Honest Capitalism is the art of leveraging your money or assets by adding value to others, while achieving a net increase in value for both of you. Money or other value, such as land holdings, precious metals, or cash in the bank, can sit around idly as stored value that might appreciate in the future. When the value is being loaned to other parties, for them to add more value, it has to potential to multiply its utility and effectiveness, to you and to others. If you have ever borrowed, loaned, or invested money, you are a capitalist. If you have done it honestly, you have leveraged capitalism to add or multiply value for yourself and/or others.

One of the most effective methods of increasing your wealth is by leveraging compound interest over time. You can accomplish this by practicing easy micro-habits such as saving five or ten percent of your earnings each month into an interest-bearing savings vehicle. Most people can live on 10 percent less than they earn, and if they invest the 10 percent wisely, they can enjoy a dramatic return in the long run.

> Capitalism can be like fire. They have both transformed mankind. Fire is good for cooking and for heating your home — but bad if it burns down your house.

Unfortunately, money can also be used as an exchange medium for cheating or stealing value from other parties. The same is true for capitalism. Capitalism can be used to multiply value that might otherwise stand idle, or it can be used to take advantage of other parties. An example of bad capitalism is when someone or an entity intentionally declares bankruptcy to avoid paying back value provided by honest workers and suppliers, or in the case of capitalism, to honest lenders. To resort to profiting from bad money or bad capitalism is a sign of weakness. It is a form of admitting that you are not competent enough to profit from providing positive value in exchange for what you can provide to other parties.

> About four years after Sun Microsystems was founded, the CEO, Scott McNealy returned to Stanford University to speak to Stanford's MBA students about how to be successful in business. Scott had co-founded Sun two years after earning his own MBA from Stanford. At the time, Sun had grown into one of the most formidable computer companies in the world — and the technology and name for Sun was purported to have come out of a project at Stanford called the "Stanford University Network."
> One of the Stanford MBA students asked Scott if he thought that it was possible for a company to become successful while being honest. Scott replied that he considered it difficult to be successful without being honest. If fact Scott said that he had recently fired one of his executives for doing something that, while not illegal, was something that Scott had considered to be unethical.
> With honesty, you build up trust and strong relationships with customers, employees and suppliers that make it easier to grow your business.

Businesses, other organizations, and entities are each Centers of their Universes too. You can increase your success with them as employees, followers, customers, or suppliers if you apply the principles of mastering their Universe.

Business

> "There is only one purpose of a business: to create a customer. A customer is defined as a

person who pays a business for goods and services. The purpose of business is to create and keep a customer."
   Peter Drucker (1909–2005), Management Consultant

THE FORMULA (OO + RRR + AA) is directly applicable to accomplishing the purpose of a business. You need to determine what kind of customer you want to create and keep, what Rewards in the form of goods and services you will offer to the customer, then you need to Act by delivering the goods and service along with Assessing how to continue to grow your customer base.

When you are creating a plan for your business, you should expand your analysis of Objectives and Options to include objectives such as financial objectives, market penetration, target markets, referenceable customers, channels, and ecosystems partners. Think about your strengths and weaknesses — your threats, risks, and opportunities. Establish goals and milestones to make it easier to Assess your progress and adjust your plan as needed. Consider the potential Reactions that you might elicit with each option — the Rewards and Results that could impact customers, partners, competitors, investors, your team, and other effected parties. There are many tools and templates available for creating a viable and compelling business plan that includes these components.

There are many functions within a business that should be monitored and measured by how effectively they help accomplish the purpose of the business. Marketing, sales, product development, manufacturing, customer support and other functions can directly affect the purpose of a business. Other functions such as finance, human resources and internal training can indirectly affect the efficiency of the primary functions — and should be measured by how much an investment in an indirect resource can save in investments in primary resources of the business. I will focus on the primary functions of a business that are the most directly impacted by the **COTU Principle**.

Leaders, Managers, and Bullies

Businesses do not typically operate effectively as democracies. Businesses thrive with strong leadership, effective management, and efficient organization.

> "If an email is sent from me with explicit directions, there are only three actions allowed by managers:
> 1. Email me back to explain why what I said was incorrect. Sometimes I'm just plain wrong!
> 2. Request further clarification if what I said was ambiguous.
> 3. Execute the directions.
> If none of the above are done, that manager will be asked to resign immediately."
> Elon Musk, (1971-), Founder and CEO of Tesla and SpaceX

The head of an organization can utilize one or many skills to be effective. Leadership and management are two types of skills employed, but there are vast differences between them. Leadership involves risk-taking and inspiring change whereas management involves risk mitigation and stability.

Leadership skills can inspire people to follow or improve their performance whereas management skills focus on keeping things running smoothly and predictably. The most effective leaders use their wisdom to decide when and how to apply leadership skills — and when to apply management techniques. They also know when to augment and organize their team with people who can add the appropriate management skills when they may be lacking in time or expertise.

If you are getting poor service in a restaurant, look at the service coverage. Sometimes you will find that the service person is working extremely hard but has too many tables to provide quality service. If this is the case, do not fault the service person — blame the management.

There are different styles of leadership and management that can be utilized depending on a subordinate or team's experience, attitudes, and the specific task involved. In the book *Management of Organizational Behavior: Utilizing Human Resources,* Paul Hersey and Kenneth H. Blanchard outline a Situational Leadership Model to assess when to apply different approaches that range from directive management, coaching, collaborating, to empowering leadership. The most effective approach depends on the person's performance readiness for a given task. A person who is highly skilled and motivated for one task may not be skilled or motivated for another task — so an accomplished leader will develop the wisdom to decide which approach is likely to be more effective.

"Never tell people how to do things. Tell them what to do and they will surprise you with their ingenuity."
George S. Patton Jr. (1885-1945), U.S. Army General

Leadership and management skill sets benefit from recognizing the differences in other people's motivations and skill sets as a consequence of the **COTU Principle** and optimizing the team member's performance by applying **THE FORMULA** to solidify your objectives and consider people's reactions based on the situation.

"It is easier to pull a string than to push it."
Proverb

Another leadership technique is bullying which involves pushing people or forcing behaviors rather than pulling to motivate a team's performance.

> At one company where I worked, we had a CEO who flew into our U.S. headquarters every week on Monday and flew out on Friday afternoon. The topic of security came up at one of our staff meetings and the CEO asked the local COO how we were handling physical security alerts on the weekends while he was away.
> The COO said that he set it up to get the alert first and check out the office before alerting the police because we would save money that way. The CEO responded by saying that it was stupid for him to take this risk and proceeded to chastise him for doing this in front of the the executive staff.

What do you think the COO thought about the CEO as a result of this interaction? What do you think the rest of the staff thought about the CEO because of this interaction? The team lost a lot of respect and loyalty for the CEO that day. If the CEO had wanted the COO and the rest of us to respect and follow him, he would have employed Engaged Thinking before acting. He could have said something like "I really respect the sacrifice that you're willing to make for the company, but your safety is much more important to me." If he had taken this approach, he would have gone a long way towards earning the team's respect and loyalty.

Bullies may have come to power by force, wealth, intimidation, family, relationships, or some other means. Sometimes people are forced to follow the directions of the bully. Sometimes they might follow a charismatic bully through effective marketing or propaganda. At other times they may follow a bully because of a lack of alternative leadership options.

> **"Hannibal Method of Motivation:** Hannibal Barca was a famous Carthaginian General who was able to invade most of the Roman Empire in 218 BC with a surprise attack that involved bringing an army with elephants across the Alps.

> There is a fable that his officers complained that the army could not make it over one of the mountains. Hannibal purportedly told them to kill every third man until they got over the mountain – and they got over the mountain."
> Business Parable

One of the dangers of bullying is that people are typically less productive when that are forced to perform than when they are motivated to perform. They are performing because of the transactional danger of not performing, instead of performing out of their own aspirational needs. Their loyalty to a bully usually wanes when they encounter a better alternative to fulfill their needs. Bullies are typically more focused on their own Universe, with little care for the people reporting to them — whereas inspirational leaders think in terms of the needs and priorities of their followers. It is worth noting that Hannibal was a military genius, but he never managed to conquer the entire Roman Empire.

> "There are four factors that determine the success of an army. Size, experience, preparation, and morale . . . and morale is more important than the other three factors combined."
> Napoleon Bonaparte (1769 – 1821), French Emperor

The Behavioral Conditioning techniques described earlier in the book are also effective in optimizing individual and group performance. A positive reinforcement reward system is an effective way to mold desired behaviors.

> "There are two things that people want more than sex and money – recognition and praise."
> Mary Kay Ash (1918 – 2001), founder of Mary Kay Cosmetics

Repetition and consistency are also important for molding behaviors. There was an article in *Harvard Business Review* that identified consistency in expected reactions from a leader as one of the strongest traits that subordinates wanted from their leaders.

> "Leadership is a potent combination of strategy and character, but if you must be without one, be without strategy."
> Norman Schwarzkopf Jr., (1934-2012) U.S. Army General

> "It's all about finding and hiring people smarter than you, getting them to join your business and giving them good work, then getting out of the way and trusting them. You have to get out of the way so you can focus on the bigger vision. That's important, but here is the main thing: You must make them see their work as a mission."
> Richard Branson, in *The Code of the Extraordinary Mind*

Leadership Skills

> "He who knows not; and knows not that he knows not, is a fool — shun him.
> He who knows not; and knows that he knows not, is learning — teach him.
> He who knows; and knows not that he knows, is sleeping — awaken him.
> He who knows; and knows that he knows, is a wise man — follow him."
> Proverb

There are several benefits and challenges to leveraging a team effort. A team can bring multiple complementary skills sets into play — but it can also introduce conflicting opinions and agendas into the equation. The diversity of players involved provides an opportunity for expanded steps to **THE FORMULA** to leverage the additional variables involved.

The Leadership Formula
THE FORMULA = OO + RRR + AA

1. Determine **Objectives & Options (OO)** – Think upfront about your objectives and options. Is this an initiative that is a priority for you, or should you delegate it to someone else? If you decide to lead the team, determine who should participate and in what roles — then establish mutuality of intent. In some cases, following your objectives might be a condition of team participation. If you poll the participants for their inputs to the objectives and listen with an open mind — you might uncover an improved set of objectives. This process also helps increase the buy-in from the other participants because they have ownership in the decision process — even if you do not end up moving forward with their suggested objectives.
2. Consider **Results, Reactions** and **Rewards (RRR)** – Think about the potential Reactions and Rewards to you, the team members, and effected parties. Again, you can gain valuable information and perspectives by polling appropriate participants and listening objectively. You can ask them to play Devil's Advocates by challenging each other's assumptions and considering alternate scenarios. Their inputs can regard their personal Reactions and Rewards, as well as those of others who might be impacted. Once an option is decided, obtain each person's commitment to the objectives, the option, the process, and the leadership. Their commitment is all the stronger if each team member commits publicly.
3. **Act** and **Assess (AA)** – A leader should be decisive. It is helpful if you can get a full agreement or consensus on the objectives and steps — but in the end, the leader should take responsibility for the decision on if, how and when to proceed. The leader

should put the plan into Action and Assess the results. Debriefing with the team can add valuable insights for future initiatives.

"A commander can be wrong, but never uncertain."
Arthur C. Clarke (1917-2008), Author, *2010: Odyssey Two*

Leaders can come from different behavioral profiles. Some leaders are best at delegating tasks to others and others lead by example. Even if the leader leads by example a successful leader can exponentially multiply their results by stimulating others into action.

"If you want to go fast, go alone. If you want to go far, go with others."
Melinda Gates (1964-), Philanthropist

Think about what success will mean to you and to your followers and the more you spread the credit and rewards, the more you will be able to influence the behavior of others.

"It is amazing what you can accomplish if you do not care who gets the credit."
Harry S. Truman (1884–1972) U. S. President

Coaching Skills

Questioning techniques and **THE FORMULA (OO + RRR + AA)** are excellent tools for coaching people who are open to listening, thinking, and being coached. The goal in coaching is to help the coaching recipient to use their brain to learn rather than simply telling them your opinion.

You can ask the recipient to describe situations that turned out well and other situations where they would like to achieve better outcomes than with their past experiences.

If you are debriefing on a previous situation, try using Deep Probing techniques. Ask at a high level what they were trying to accomplish and then probe more deeply to encourage them to dig deeper for any underlying objectives. Ask about how they felt as a result of the interaction and how they think the other person or entity reacted. What they would do differently in the future. If they were happy with the results, how would they replicate their success in the future, or even improve the future results. If they were dissatisfied with the results, ask how they could improve in the future.

You can walk the coaching recipient through **THE FORMULA** to consider how to handle future situations. If you are coaching the person outside their comfort zones, it is normal for people to not act, or delay their actions. Ask for a commitment on when they will Act next. Note that this is the same process you can use for self-coaching.

Teams also go through a meshing process that can benefit from effective coaching techniques. In 1965, Bruce Tuckman identified four phases of the team meshing process that teams typically evolve through to achieve optimal performance: **Forming, Storming, Norming and Performing**.

During the **Forming Stage**, a leader can organize team members, help the team agree on the common objectives, and identify opportunities and challenges towards achieving the team objectives. This is a stage where the leader focus on *coordinating team behaviors*.

In the **Storming Stage** of team development, team members start to identify each other's opinions, strengths, weaknesses, hierarchies, and behavioral styles — and conflicts can emerge. Sometimes conflicts remain unresolved, and those teams end up underperforming without evolving out of the Storming Stage and into optimal Norming and Performing Stages. Other teams may naturally mesh smoothly and jump directly to the Norming Stage. During the Storming Stage, the leader should focus on *coaching behaviors* within the team.

The **Norming Stage** is when the team learns how to resolve conflicts and work towards common objectives. This is a stage where the leader should focus on *empowering behaviors*.

The **Performing Stage** is when the team is operating at optimal efficiency and when the leader can focus on *supporting behaviors*. Note: one-to-one relationships often need to evolve through the same **Forming-Storming-Norming-Performing Stages**.

A technique to speed up and smooth a team through these developmental phases is to lead the team through team building and trust developing exercises. These exercises can involve team problem solving exercises which draw out potential conflicts — while solving challenges which are not relevant to the actual team objectives. The goal is facilitating the team's transition into a high-performance team mode that can be applied towards achieving the real team objectives.

It helps speed up the bonding process if you can find exercises that are fun for the team to accomplish together. There are several packaged exercises, like desert and arctic survival tests that create a scenario that requires a team to agree upon a priority of items from a list that has been provided. Other tests include more physical exercises like trusting team mates to guide participants through an obstacle course.

The coach can debrief the team after the exercises to help the team identify behaviors that can be applied to help the team perform more effectively towards accomplishing the real team objectives.

Mentoring and coaching others can be very self-fulfilling. The gratitude and success of your recipients can provide the rewards to satisfy your high-level Maslow's Pyramid needs and help condition your positive behaviors in the future.

Public Speaking Skills

Public Speaking is one of the greatest fears of mankind! Even an experienced public speaker can be intimidated if they have not spoken publicly for a while.

> "All of the great speakers were bad speakers at first."
> Ralph Waldo Emerson (1803-1882), Author

There are many forms of one-to-many communications such as broadcasting on radio or TV, posting on social networks, or writing a book. Most of us will have occasion to speak publicly, whether it is in a formal presentation or asking a question in a group situation like a classroom. Accordingly, I will focus on public speaking as a form of one-to-many communications in this section of the book. I will touch upon some other forms of communication in the Sales and Marketing Addendum, and I suggest exploring other forms independently if you have an interest.

> Reframe nervousness into excitement! Excitement is full of positive energy.

You will be more effective in all forms of one-to-many communications if you apply the three steps in **THE FORMULA**. You are overlapping with multiple people's Universes for a short period of time and should try to make it as beneficial for them as possible. **THE FORMULA** applies towards determining and executing on your content for a presentation.

Master The Universe Formula
THE FORMULA = OO + RRR + AA

1. **OO** – Determine your Objectives and Options.
2. **RRR** – Consider potential Results, Reactions, and Rewards to determine your course of action.
3. **AA** – Act and Assess.

PRO TIP: Use the condensed acronym **"ORA"** to remember **THE FORMULA.**

When preparing for public speaking, determine what you want to accomplish and then try to consider it through the lenses of the audience's Universe. The audience is asking themselves some of the same questions you ask when you are listening to a speaker. What am I going to get out of this and what is my reward for listening? Why am I spending my time here? Is this worth my time and is this someone that I should take seriously? What do you expect me to know or do differently at the end of the talk, etc.? Think about how these questions apply to the topic and content of the talk.

Think about how you are going to open the talk in a way to capture their interest and help answer these questions for them? Are you setting their expectations on the objectives of the talk? For example, tell them what you are going to tell them (the introduction), tell them (the body of the talk), and then tell them what you told them (summarize at the end of the talk to reinforce the message).

Pick up to three main points that you'd like the audience to remember. You have done a good job if they remember one of the points, a great job if they remember all three points and an outstanding job if they remember even more. Use the power of repetition to highlight these points and the beginning, throughout, and during the summary of the talk.

It is also useful to set any logistical expectations at the beginning of the talk, like how long you are going to spend, will you take questions during the talk, or if there will be time for questions at the end of the talk. Setting these expectations will reduce distracting questions from their minds throughout your talk.

Public Speaking Tips:

1. **Master yourself** – Prepare beforehand and use breathing and mindfulness techniques to ground yourself.
2. **Set the stage** – Set reward expectations and establish rapport.
3. **Master the space** – Leverage the Power of the Pause.
4. **Engage** – Connect and relate to the audience's Universe(s).
5. **Summarize** – Key points and call to action.

Master yourself – Repetition will make you more comfortable with public speaking. Practice the talk as often as possible prior to the event and you will be more comfortable and natural when you step in front of the audience. You will be able to focus more on the moment instead of the next sentence. It helps to create a brief outline of a few key points you want to cover and their sequence. It is much easier to remember only three or four primary messages than to memorize a whole presentation. In that way, you can create more space in your mind to focus on the moment and have a more natural and credible discussion with the audience.

Before and during the talk, you can employ some of the techniques discussed earlier to get control of your Universe and be more effective. You can practice breathing or other meditation techniques to center yourself before the talk. You have already invested time and attention considering the audience's Universes and now it is time to focus on yourself. Even if you only have a few moments to prepare for a talk, or even a public comment, you can perform some deep breathing exercises before jumping into the speaking session.

You can also apply the NLP sensory overloading technique used in the Fire Walk, as described in Section 2 to

How To MASTER THE UNIVERSE
Personal and Professional Life-Skills Guide

help calm any anxiety or negative emotions. Focus on visual sights and auditory sounds to minimize unwanted emotional influences.

Positive emotional influences, like excitement about the topic or speaking experience are good and can help create a more rewarding and entertaining experience — for you and the audience.

> "Act enthusiastic and you will be enthusiastic."
> Dale Carnegie (1888-1955) Self-improvement author

Set the stage - Start building rapport and setting expectations early in your talk. Clearly identify the objectives and the benefits — or rewards for the audience. Try to tap into their emotions in a positive way early and often during the presentation.

> **Entertain:** to hold the attention.
> *Dictionary.com*

If you cannot hold the audience's attention, why would they listen to your talk? So, you need to entertain them. This does not mean that you should make a joke when covering a serious topic. It does mean that you should do your best to get the audience's attention from the beginning of the talk, maintain their attention throughout the talk, and close with a memorable summary and if appropriate, a compelling call-to-action.

> Every time I have seen the Rolling Stones band perform in person, I have been amazed at the energy Mick Jagger and the band put into the concert. It's as if Mick gathers the band together before each concert with a pep talk about how this is going to be the best concert they have ever given — even though they have performed the same songs hundreds of times before.
> Likewise, when the comedian Steve Martin tells

a joke that he has told hundreds of times before, it is no longer funny to Steve Martin, but he makes it fresh and funny for the audience.

Master the Space - During the talk, it is important to take time to pause between the points you are making. Create some Space — for yourself and for the audience. Take a moment for a deep breath or two between points. This accomplishes a few objectives. From the audience's perspective, they have time to think and to process the previous point, instead of having it be a distraction from your next point. A pause receives more attention from an audience than rapid-fire talking — you are creating a vacuum that builds their anticipation for what you are going to say next. A pause makes you appear to be in control to the audience and you will be more in control. And finally, it gives you time to relax, gather your thoughts, and confidently proceed with the rest of the talk.

> If you watch the speech Malala made to the United Nations in 2013 on her 16th birthday, you will see some great examples of her creating space and anticipation with the power of the pause during a speech.

Depending on the venue, you can keep the attention of the audience by walking calmly and purposefully around the stage or room between points you are making — stopping at different locations while making your points. Or you can walk excitedly if you want to spark more attention. You can also mix up your pace to create emphasis on key points. Your movement around the venue will help keep the audience's attention and keep them more alert in case they become the focus of your next stop to make a point. Conversely, if you constantly pace and never stop to talk at a given point(s), you will be distracting to the audience and appear nervous at the same time.

If you are using any props like slides or a flip board, never talk to the prop — talk to the audience. For example, if you are discussing a bullet on the slide, touch or point to it and then turn to talk directly to the audience.

Engage - Pick out one person to look at and talk with at a time, as if you are talking one-to-one at each stopping point. Look that one person in the eyes when you are talking to them. It is easier to talk to one person than a whole room. And from the perspective of the surrounding audience members, it will appear as if you are talking directly to them too. Cover a point or so with that one person, and then move on to another person.

If appropriate, try to engage the audience by asking them questions or getting them to react, but be prepared for how you want to handle their responses.

Carefully planted repetition can help get the audience's attention and reinforce key points. You can occasionally repeat a phrase to call attention to it. For example, you can make a statement like "This policy is going to change our air quality for life," pause and then repeat the phrase. You can also intersperse a phrase at different points in the presentation to help create familiarity and recollection of the phrase. Just make sure that you do not overdue the repetition to the point of annoyance or boredom.

> "Make sure you have finished speaking before your audience has finished listening."
> Dorothy Sarnoff (1914 – 2008) Singer and Actress

Summarize – Finish the session by reviewing the key messages from your talk — and any next steps that you will provide for the audience or suggest to them. Also, summarize the benefits or rewards to the audience.

These are a few tips, and there are many books, special interest groups and courses available on the topic of public speaking. The more you practice, and the more feedback and coaching you have — the better and more comfortable you will get with public speaking.

Public speaking can even become fun! Afterall, if you're the speaker you have the mandate of the Universe over the room, the timing, the agenda, your movement, and even the thermostat. Whereas participants are usually stuck in a seat, at the mercy of the speaker.

> "Do the thing you fear most, and the death of fear is certain."
> Mark Twain (1835 – 1910) American author

Negotiation Skills

> **Negotiation**: mutual discussion and arrangement of the terms of a transaction or agreement
> *Dictionary.com*

We all negotiate, whether in our personal or business lives. Some discussions and agreements may be contractual, and others may be verbal. Spouses negotiate with each other on issues like daily activities or major life choices. Parents negotiate with their children — and vice-a-versa. Friends negotiate with each other on dinner plans. We even negotiate with ourselves regarding our priorities and rewards for our actions.

There are often benefits to putting major agreements in writing. A written agreement can clarify responsibilities and expectations and reduce the potential for misunderstanding or memory lapses. In the case of an organizational agreement, a contract can memorialize the terms if any of the negotiators are not involved in the future.

Think about the steps of **THE FORMULA** when preparing for a negotiation. What are your Objectives and Options, and what are the desired Results and Rewards for you and the other party? One way to help clarify expectations of a simple verbal agreement is to have both parties repeat back to the other their understanding of the agreement.

Sales often end up with a negotiation and probing is an important step in the negotiating process — just as it is in the sales process. If this is true in your situation, start incorporating negotiation related fact-finding research and probing early in your sales process. Use Deep Probing to try to identify what negotiation points are most important to your prospect and which ones can be points of commonality. Also, assess what terms are more important to you and which ones are optional. Try to sort out a way to make the agreement a win-win for both parties.

> Early in my career, I worked on closing a deal to sell a record-breaking number of engineering workstations to the largest semiconductor company in the world. I was only 25 years old and for the final step of the sales process I had to meet with the head of purchasing.
> For this large of a deal with such an elite customer, he said that I should be offering them a larger than normal volume discount.
> I asked him if he knew how much it cost their company for every day's delay in product development. He didn't know the answer. I knew the answer and respectfully explained how his company was going to improve their time-to-market, revenues and profits using our products — and how the standard volume discount was a good deal for them and a good deal for us.
> It was a win-win for both companies — and he ended up agreeing to our standard volume discount prices.

Consider the other parties' alternatives to coming to an agreement. This is often referred to as the **BATNA** – the **B**est **A**lternative **T**o a **N**egotiated **A**greement. What do you think is their **BATNA**? Also, what is your **BATNA**? At what point would you be willing to walk away from an agreement. It is hard to negotiate if you are not willing to walk away under certain circumstances.

> I helped my brother purchase a plot of land next to a home that I owned several years ago. A developer purchased land uphill from our properties and the developer approached me about paying my brother for an easement through his lot to run a sewage line through his property to connect to the main sewer line.
>
> This didn't sound very attractive to my brother, and I estimated that it would be very costly for the developer to route the pipeline elsewhere. The developers **BATNA** was much more expensive than the cost of purchasing my brother's lot to run the line — and then resell the lot.
>
> I went back to the developer and told him "No" to the easement, but my brother would accept a property sales price that was 60% higher than he paid two years prior to that time. The developer finally accepted the proposal.
>
> This negotiation ended up as a win-win for the developer and my brother – much more of a win for my brother than if we had not considered the developer's **BATNA**. It is also an example of establishing a pricing model where the price was based on the value to the other party instead of the cost of the property.

It is more of a win for the other party if you can help the other party feel better about the negotiation. You might want an ongoing relationship with the other party to encourage repeat business and referrals.

> "You get more with a kind word and a gun than you get with just a kind word."
> Willie Sutton (1901-1980), American Bank Robber

The converse of this quote often applies as well. You get more with a kind word and a gun than you get with just a gun. I've gone into negotiations where I clearly had the upper hand and won over the other party and established a strong long-term relationship by being friendly in the process.

One approach to winning a negotiation or competitive situation is to use the P-A-R-T-S technique to change the game, as described in the section on Winning. Here is an example of changing the rules of a negotiation from the other party's rules to your own rules.

> Early in a negotiation with a major Japanese company, I had informed them that our prices were increasing after the end of our company's financial year. The client agreed to this timeline.
>
> Then, on the last day of the financial year, the client informed me that the Japanese have what they call a "Ringi Process" where major purchase orders are circulated and then formally presented to the senior manager for signing at the end of the month. They explained that this would happen at 5 P.M. Tokyo time, which was 1 A.M the next morning in my company's time zone. This would be in my company's next financial year.
>
> Instead of playing by their rules, I respectfully said that we had our own form of "Ringi Process." Our process meant that the prices went up at the stroke of midnight, our time. They found a way to get the purchase order signed just before midnight our time.

Sometimes the timing of the deal or the timing of a compromise or concession on a deal can improve the other party's satisfaction.

> I once negotiated a $225M net-present-value, company-wide licensing agreement with a Fortune 100 company. I knew that the other company's CEO wanted to announce the licensing deal prior to a major trade show the following week and I told the negotiators know that my CEO had informed me that negotiating the right deal was more important to us than closing the deal by the trade show. Consequently, I put all the deadline pressure on the other party.
>
> Also, licensing rights to one of the product lines was not critical to my company and my CEO had

told me I could offer this concession for free in the beginning of the negotiation. I held out on offering this concession until the final day of their decision deadline when we wanted them to also agree to another final term. Then I told them that I needed to make a private call to my CEO to discuss this final compromise.

When I returned to the room to tell them that we agreed to the concessions, they were so happy that they "high-fived" each other. By waiting until then end of the negotiation for this concession, I was able to trade it for another concession and they felt that they had been more successful with the negotiated agreement.

Sales Skills

We all sell — and we all buy!

This is true whether we are selling products, plans or ideas. We even sell to ourselves when we want to talk ourselves into a decision.

People hate to be "sold to" — but they love to "buy."

One of the challenges is that most people have trouble making decisions — and they do not like to feel forced or manipulated into a decision. They cringe at the thought of going into a dealership to buy a car and having a salesperson push them into spending their hard-earned money. But if a salesperson focuses on their client's Universe and what they are trying to accomplish, the salesperson can become a problem-solving ally by helping them "make a decision." A key to effective selling is to put yourself into the other party's Universe and adapt your mentality towards helping them buy and make decisions — instead of "selling" to them by pushing a solution.

Selling is the art of helping someone "make a decision."

One approach to understanding a prospect's objectives is to simply ask them why they would want your solution.

When I worked at Sun Microsystems, I headed up the sales and business development effort to launch a new technology called JavaCard. One of the most important companies we needed to partner with to make the initiative successful was the credit card company Visa International. To help facilitate the relationship, we arranged for a strategic meeting between the CEO of Visa and the CEO of the JavaSoft subsidiary of Sun.

In preparation for the CEO meeting, we met with a senior executive at Visa. At the start of the meeting, I asked the executive why he thought that JavaCard was important to Visa. He went up to a whiteboard and started outlining the benefits to Visa. After about ten minutes, he stopped, looked at me and said, "aren't you the one who is supposed to be selling the benefits to me." I smiled and said that he was doing a much better job than I ever could have done. So, he continued outlining more benefits to Visa and the market.

We went on to sign an agreement with Visa and 20 of the largest smart card manufacturers representing around 95% of the market. The JavaCard technology has since been licensed to run on tens of billions of products including credit cards, mobile phone chip cards, transportation, security, and medical products — making it arguably the most ubiquitous operating platform in the history of computing.

There was a study published in the Harvard Business Review that identified empathy and ego drive as the two most common traits of successful salespeople. Empathy involves respecting the **COTU Principle** — appreciating that everyone is the Center of their own Universe. The study points out that the empathy trait was not to be confused with sympathy. The successful salespeople tried to understand the prospect's perspective but did not need to agree with it. For example, if a prospect said that they did not like a particular attribute of a solution, the salesperson might respond with something like "I understand that this is a concern for you. What features of a solution are the most important to you?" In this way, the salesperson is respecting the prospect's Universe and probing for more information. The ego drive trait helps the sales overcome objections and drive towards a successful sale.

Two of the greatest attributes of a successful salesperson are humility and enthusiasm.

In this section, the focus will be on one-to-one selling, as opposed to one-to-many selling in a marketing campaign. There are common elements to a typical one-to-one sales process.

Sales Process:

1. **Prospecting** - Finding potential clients.
2. **Qualifying** - Identifying the potential for a sale.
3. **Probing** - Questioning to identify the perceived issues, benefits, and decision processes for a prospect.
4. **Presenting** - Explaining or demonstrating the benefits to the prospect.
5. **Overcoming objections** - Reducing obstacles to the sale.
6. **Closing** - Securing a decision to move forward.

"If you don't ask, you don't get it."
Mahatma Gandhi (1869-1948), Indian Civil Rights Leader

Prospecting - There are several methods to find prospective customers. You can knock on doors, make phone calls, send emails, use social media, and leverage mass-marketing to contact your prospects. These activities will be more efficient if you take the time to research and learn as much as you can about the prospect before contacting them — and then target your prospecting efforts to prospects who fit a more likely profile for your products or solutions. Prospects who have not been qualified to fit ideal sales profiles are often labeled "Suspects" instead of "Prospects" for forecasting purposes.

> A salesperson calculated that it required calling an average of 50 prospects to make a $20,000 sale worth $1,000 in commissions. She wanted to close $200,000 of sales and make $10,000 in commissions a month. To accomplish this commission rate, she set a goal of at least 500 calls a month – which is 125 calls a week.
>
> She calculated that every call she made was worth $20 on average — so to keep herself motivated, after every call she celebrated and told herself that she just rewarded herself with $20 — whether she closed a sale on that particular sales call or not.

Qualifying – Evaluate how much time, expense, and effort you should be investing in pursuing a prospect? **MANOT** is an acronym for a set of qualifying criteria in a sales process. You can think of it as an abbreviation for whether a prospect "may" or "may not" be a qualified sales target.

Basic Qualification Criteria (MANOT):

1. **M**oney - Does the prospect have the funding for the purchase?
2. **A**uthority - Does the prospect have the authority to make the decision? If not, who has the decision-making authority?

3. **Need** - Is there a perceived or potential need for the product?
4. **Objections** (or **Obstacles**) - What are the hurdles involved?
5. **Timing** - What is the anticipated decision timeframe for the prospect?

> **PRO TIP:** You can reorganize the sequence of the questions based on priorities or appropriateness throughout your interactions with the prospect. You can then track probabilities and estimated timeframes to each criterion when developing a forecasting sales funnel.

A skilled salesperson should probe to understand why the prospect might be in the market for the salesperson's products. The salesperson should probe to discover what problems the client had that he or she might be able to help solve and ask for reference to other prospects who might have a solvable problem. In the end, if the prospect does not fit the qualification criteria, the salesperson should reprioritize their time towards finding more qualified prospects.

Perform as much qualifying of your prospects prior to contacting them to improve your sales funnel process and then use your probing skills to qualify them further when you start having direct interactions with them. You might even decide not to pursue a prospect due to factors such as their close relationship with a competitor, their legal, ethical, or financial reputation.

Probing – Ask open-ended, probing questions to qualify the prospect and get a first-hand understanding if their objectives and priorities. Remember the second step of **THE FORMULA, 2**. Consider Results, Reactions and Rewards **(RRR)**. Instead of guessing at their perceived rewards — you can simply ask them.

> You'd be surprised by how much someone will tell you if you're not afraid to ask the right questions.

There is a Deep Probing, qualifying process developed by Neil Rackam called **SPIN Selling** which involves a layered process of to identify the benefits or rewards for the prospect.

SPIN Selling:

1. **S**ituation – Ask the prospect about their current situation. What products or solutions are they currently using?
2. **P**roblem – What challenges are the prospect encountering in the current situation?
3. **I**mplication – What is the impact of continuing with the current solutions? E.g., How is it affecting their profitability, competitiveness, efficiency, and customer satisfaction?
4. **N**eed – Ask what the prospect thinks that they would Need to solve the problems and mitigate the negative implications of their current approach — and the payoff or benefit of the new approach.

Keep in mind that the prospect is the Center of their Universe and some of their most important objectives are personal. You might want to tactfully probe to discover how the decision might affect their career, recognition, job satisfaction, or any other personal objectives.

When you ask the question, shut up — pause to give the prospect time to answer. Utilize your active listening skills, and do not interrupt the other party.

> As a young salesperson — when I asked a question, I would shut up and calmly count the seconds in my head before the other person responded. They were eventually compelled to fill the space — and they always responded!

Ask about the prospect about the process they used for their last major purchasing decision. Was it an analytical or a relationship-oriented process? Did they need a lot of details, or did they need to demo or trial to experience the solution? Did they use NLP related Visual, Auditory, or Kinesthetic terms while describing the process? If they used multiple NLP modalities, what sequence did they follow? Ask if they were happy with the process and how the process would have been improved. When presenting, try to accommodate a process and terminology that is most comfortable for the prospect.

Presenting – A salesperson should try to understand their prospect's perceived needs before presenting a solution or attempting to close the sale. Every feature that a salesperson mentions to a prospect should always be accompanied with a benefit statement — explaining why this feature could be important to the prospect. Try to relate it back to how it will help them survive or thrive.

Make the effort to use the pacing and leading process that was discussed in the section on **Meshing and Rapport**. Try to use the same terminology and a similar rate of speech as the prospect. If the pacing is different than your normal approach, it may feel a little awkward to you — but it will feel comfortable to the customer and improve your rapport.

> "It is easier to sell expectations than to sell excuses."
> Business Proverb

When you propose a solution to a prospect, it is important to set realistic expectations for many reasons. It takes work and time to acquire a customer and repeat customers are easier to sell to than new ones. Building trust is important for building a repeat relationship. Another reason is that it takes more time and effort to rationalize excuses than it does to set expectations upfront.

> Early in my career I helped one of the largest tech companies (at the time) develop an account management course. I decided to research the requirements by interviewing decision makers at their largest customers. Instead of providing a list

of options, I asked them open-ended questions to identify the important characteristics of a good account manager from their perspectives.

The most consistent answer that I received was — honesty and responsiveness. They wanted to be told the truth in a timely fashion. For example, if a delivery was going to be delayed, they wanted to know the truth as soon as possible so that they could plan around it. They know that delays happen, and they don't like it — but it is even worse if they are told too late. This can help build a trust and bonding relationship with the customer for the future.

Another time I took over the account management responsibilities for one of our company's largest accounts. When I met the primary decision maker for the first time, he said that my predecessor had lied to him and asked why he should trust me. I suggested that there was probably nothing I could say to convince him that I was trustworthy, other than asking him to give me a chance. He agreed, I earned his trust and never lost a sale to another competitor for the rest of my tenure with that account.

Overcoming objections – Use your Deep Probing skills to uncover any potential obstacles to the decision process. Try to turn it into a joint problem-solving process. You can even directly ask the prospect what would keep them from proceeding.

Some objections can be overcome by qualifying the importance of the objection. Use Deep Probing to uncover the most important objections. For example, if a client objects to one attribute of the solution, a skilled salesperson might ask whether the prospect would move forward if that attribute was not an issue. If the prospect gave a second, third or fourth objection, the salesperson could keep going through the same process until uncovering the most important objection. Many times, the earliest objections are smokescreens to avoid making decisions — so focus on the final objection. Ask if the prospect would move forward if you could overcome that objection. If not, ask what would be required for the prospect to move forward.

A possible next step is to ask the prospect which of the concerns were most important, and then ask the prospect what attributes were most desirable to the prospect — then work through a pro and con decision process.

Closing - The final and most important part of the sales process is closing the sale — helping the customer "make a decision."

> The top late-night talk show host years ago was Johnny Carson. One night, Johnny hosted Fred Herman, who was touted as America's Greatest Salesman.
> Johnny said, "OK, you're supposed to be a good salesman. Sell me something."
> Fred said, "what would you like me to sell you?"
> Johnny looked around, selected an ashtray on his desk and said, "Sell me this ashtray."
> Fred asked, "why might you want to own an ashtray like this?"
> Johnny gave a few reasons and Fred responded with "It sounds like having an ashtray is very important to you. How much would you be willing to pay for it?"
> Johnny said, "25 cents", to which Fred closed with "OK Johnny, I'll let you have it for that."

The more you practice multi-level, Deep Probing, the easier it will be to uncover the perceived rewards for the client. Fred probed with open-ended questions — questions that are not easily answered with yes-no responses. He probed to uncover an immediate need and the specific importance to the prospect. And then he probed the value of a solution to the prospect. Finally, Fred made it easy for Johnny to "make a decision."

There are many techniques to closing a sale. You can ask a question that requires an easier decision. For instance, you can ask when the prospect would like to have delivery, and then turn the discussion into a joint problem-solving discussion on how to coordinate the paperwork and delivery process.

Asking when a client wants delivery before even asking for the final purchase decision is also a form of an assumptive close. You are establishing an assumption that the prospect with be making a purchasing decision that will require a delivery. An assumptive close is a technique that many children learn at an early age.

You can ask trial closing questions as you go through the whole sales process to gage your progress and create a habit of making easier decisions before asking for the final decision. Persistence is a common attribute of most successful salespeople.

> I was at a bar with some friends when one of the single men went to ask a woman to dance — and she refused him.
> When our friend returned to the group, he became the subject of some teasing from some of the others.
> He just smiled and said, "No's don't count — only yes's count." He continued to ask women to dance and ended up with more success than his friends.

It is true that only the yes's count, but two of your sales goals should be to improve your closing ration and optimize your time. Good selling skills will help improve the number of yes's you get. In summary, attempt to increase the number of sales you close, increase the size of your average sale and/or reduce the timeframes of your sales cycles.

From an overall business management perspective, assigning probabilities, values, and timeframes to these stages for a particular product and business provide a foundation for sales projections and investment planning for each of the specific stages.

You can track your closing ratios of sales calls to the sales that you close and even track it by steps in the Sales Process.

You can refine your data based on specific metrics such as number of mailers, phone calls, face-to-face meetings, demonstrations, verbal agreements, and even milestones in the client's procurement process. For example, you might discover that only 90% of purchase requisitions to the procurement department end up as orders. You can then use the tracking data to make decisions on where and how to improve the process. By tracking this sales funnel, you can assess your projected success rate based on the number of events in each of the steps — and use this as a metric to determine how to increase the funnel size and/or speed.

Do not be afraid to ask someone to trust you with their business. You are doing them a favor if you are helping them make decisions to help solve problems or achieve greater success. You can achieve your sales Objectives and Options **(OO)** more easily if you keep the client's interests in mind **(RRR)** and help make it easier for them make decisions **(AA)**.

> "He's a man way out there in the blue, riding on a smile and a shoeshine... A salesman is got to dream, boy. It comes with the territory."
> *Death of a Salesman*, by Arthur Miller (1915-2005)

Marketing Skills

Marketing involves the identification, definition, and/or creation of business opportunities and the demand for goods and services — which I will generically refer to as products. Marketing functions are sometimes segmented in various disciplines including Product Management, Product Marketing, and Marketing Communications. All of these functions rely upon a concept called Knowing Your Customer (KYC), which directly relates back to the **COTU**

Principle — knowing what customers will value in the product to survive and/or thrive. Then applying **THE FORMULA (OO + RRR + AA).**

> "The aim of marketing is to know and understand the customer so well the product or service fits him and sells itself."
> "The aim of marketing is to make selling superfluous."
> Peter Drucker (1909 – 2005), Management Consultant

Product Management deals with identifying potential new products based on existing market needs or identifying trends that will lead to new product opportunities. Product managers have responsibilities for determining target markets, product components and specifications, business justifications, costing, pricing, forecasting, and overall Product Lifecycle Management (PLM).

> "Two shoe companies sent marketeers to do research on a primitive island. One reported back that there was no market opportunity because no one on the island wore shoes. The other marketeer reported that there was a huge opportunity because no one was wearing shoes yet."
> Business Proverb

> "I skate to where the puck is going to be, not where it has been."
> Wayne Gretzky (1961-), Ice Hockey Player and Coach

Determining target markets involves identifying profiles for target customers to determine what features to prioritize for inclusion in the product and for promotion to customers. A life cycle Return on Investment (ROI) business plan for the product should identify the investment stages along with the overall ROI for the product. It should include the types of investments such as design, development, production, product marketing, business systems requirements, product launch, marketing communications, delivery, sales, and support.

Price Determination (CACS):

1. **C**ost – What will it cost you to develop, build, and deliver the product or solution?
2. **A**dded Value – What is the product worth to the customer? What will they get in return for using it or what will they lose for not using your product?
3. **C**ompetition – How much are competitors pricing comparable products? Competition can come from third party sources, from the customer developing their own alternatives, or it can come from the customer doing nothing.
4. **S**trategic Value – Is there a strategic benefit to offering customers a product at a lower margin or even offering it at a loss? Examples include customer references, intellectual property value, customer acquisition value, establishing business relationships for selling other products, upselling opportunities for upgrades or change orders.

Pricing and marketing based on Added Value to the customer should help achieve higher profit margins. If your Costs are higher than the Added Value to the customer, your competitor's pricing, and the Strategic Value to you — you should reconsider the benefits of developing or continuing the product.

> "Quality in a product or service is not what the supplier puts in. It is what the customer gets out and is willing to pay for. A product is not quality because it is hard to make and costs a lot of money, as manufacturers typically believe. This is incompetence. Customers pay only for what is of use to them and gives them value. Nothing else constitutes quality."

> "Because the purpose of business is to create a customer, the business enterprise has two—and only two—basic functions: marketing and innovation, marketing and innovation produce results; all the rest are costs. Marketing is the distinguishing, unique function of the business."
> Peter Drucker (1909–2005), Management Consultant

Product Marketing forms a bridge between Product Management and Marketing Communications. This function clarifies the problem and/or opportunity the product addresses, the target market segment, market sizing, value proposition to the target prospects and customers, competitive positioning, pricing, and sales channels.

Whereas Product Management and Product Marketing determine the profile of target customers, Marketing Communications (Marcom) is responsible for delivering the communication channels and messages to influence customers to purchase the products. The communication channels can include direct marketing, indirect channels through third parties, online marketing, advertising, and public relations.

> "A compelling story, even if factually inaccurate, can be more emotionally compelling than a dry recitation of the truth."
> Frank Luntz (1962-), GOP strategist

Profiling target customers and messaging to them involves understanding what drives the customers behaviors — how target customers can perceive surviving and/or thriving via the purchase of the product. To accomplish this, you should determine what the customer desires to satisfy needs at one or more levels of Maslow's Hierarchy of Needs. Do you want to appeal to the target customer's Physiological Needs, Safety Needs, Social Needs, Self Esteem Needs, and/or Self Actualization Needs?

> "I suppose that Willie had his natural quota of ordinary suspicion and caginess, but those things tend to evaporate when what people tell you is what you want to hear."
> *All the King's Men*, by Robert Penn Warren
> (1905-1989)

People are driven to address their Physiological Needs to survive and thrive. They are anthropologically programmed by their Safety and Social Needs to want to belong to and be accepted by a tribe or group. You can appeal to your target customer's fears or their aspirations. Purchasing habits can be stimulated by psychological fears such as Fear of Missing Out (FOMO) where people do not want to be left out of their group's activities — or by the fear of physical threats, like pain avoidance through medications. There is safety and security in numbers and people are motivated to follow marketing that addresses these needs. People also want to satisfy their Self-Esteem and Self Actualization Needs.

> The CEO of one of the early online game companies told me that the secret to making a game addictive is to make it aspirational. Even when a player fails to win or achieve the next level in a game, make it seem like the player has the potential and ability to win or achieve the next level.

You can also appeal to a customer's Reflexive thinking and put them into a state of cognitive ease by associating your product with attractive images and aspirations.

> Fragrance commercials usually try to appeal to an aspirational life or state of mind without ever describing the smell of their product.

Marketing techniques can be used to promote ideologies, concepts, political agendas, and religions as well as commercial products. Repetition of your messaging makes the message more familiar and less threatening — which in turn makes it more believable and persuasive to the customer. Repetition and familiarity put minds into a state of cognitive ease, which appeals to the Reflexive Thinking process.

Be wary of being tricked into believing falsehoods yourself — based on marketing efforts that set your mind into a state of cognitive ease.

> "If you tell a big enough lie and tell it frequently enough, it will be believed."
> Adolf Hitler (1989-1945), German Dictator

> "A lie told once is still a lie, but a lie told 1000 times becomes the truth."
> Rumored to be from Hitler's propagandist,
> Joseph Goebbels

I do not condone lying. I believe in honest marketing. I think that lying is a sign of weakness and causes damage to your Karma Pool. These last two quotes demonstrate the power of repetition — even when applied to obvious lies. Honest marketing might take some more effort, but it will feed your Karma Pool and can be used as a foundation for creating loyal customers.

Most products have strengths and weaknesses depending on the perspective and profile of the customer. Highlight the positive aspects and benefits of your product to your target customers. If you have applied the **COTU Principle** to know your customer and you have created an appropriate product — you should be able to market to customers with integrity.

Effective marketing may not always "make selling superfluous" as with Peter Drucker's aim of marketing, but it can make selling significantly easier. In the book *Virtual Selling*, Thomas Siebel introduces the concept of Zero-Defect Selling to be analogous to Zero-Defect (ZD)

Manufacturing. Zero Defect Manufacturing emphasizes that quality control in one stage of manufacturing can have as much as a ten times improvement and cost savings in downstream stages of a manufacturing process. A worse-case scenario is to not correct a defect until after the product has ended up with a customer. This is true whether ZD is applied to the manufacturing or the marketing/selling process. In either case you want to avoid the added downstream costs and the negative impacts on customer satisfaction.

> I once worked for a company that sold laptop computers to engineers. At one point we started having customers complain that the computers were heating up so much that they were to hold on their laps. The CEO was the creator of the computer and claimed that the customers must be wrong because his computer was not overheating.
> We finally discovered that our supplier of heat sensors had switched from Fahrenheit to Celsius based sensors without telling us. This proved that the customers were right — our computers were overheating. If the computer's processor was expected to slow down at 86 degrees in Fahrenheit, 86 degrees with the Celsius sensors translated to not slowing down until the processor exceeded 186 degrees Fahrenheit.

This is an example of the value of listening to and valuing the opinions of your customers. Catching this problem after the product was in our customers' hands proved much more costly than catching it and correcting it at an earlier manufacturing stage.

In a Zero-Defect Selling example, marketing is a stage that should be more heavily invested in than the selling stage to make the selling process more efficient. An effective investment in marketing can have a multiplier effect on the effectiveness of your sales activities.

Added Value

Every organizational function is important if it can justify its added value versus other functions in the organization. For example, if the headcount and costs of a training department can make the company proportionally more productive than the cost of the constituents that they are training, then the training department's value is justified. If a hospital administrative staffer frees up enough time for a medical professional to earn more than the cost of the staffer, then the value if the staffer is justified. It is a good practice to try to add value in every interaction — internally and externally.

Whether you are working for an entity, be it a non-profit, a for profit, or directly for a client, or for yourself — the **COTU Principle** applies. Consider how you can Add Value to the entity and learn from the Results of your Actions.

> **COTU Principle:** Every entity is the Center of its own Universe and is motivated by its own survival and success.

What is your Added Value? Think about how the entity might benefit through the second step in **THE FORMULA (OO + RRR + AA)**. Consider Results, Reactions, and Rewards **(RRR)** as they affect the other party. For a given Objective — what are the potential Reactions and Rewards for you, the client and/or the entity? Are the rewards in the form of profits, customer satisfaction, repeat or referenceable business, personal satisfaction, career progressions, recognition, employment continuation, or some other form?

> I was once hosting a visitor at the original Ghirardelli Ice Cream and Chocolate Shop in San Francisco when I notice that the table next to me was covered with gobs of left-over ice cream and

syrup. When the waiter came to clean the table, I asked him, "don't you hate people like that?" He smiled and replied, "If it wasn't for people like that, I wouldn't have a job."

I try to remember this experience and the positive attitude of the waiter whenever I have faced challenging professional situations. Challenges are often opportunities to Add Value.

Try to add value with all of your interactions. Keep in mind that money is only one measure of Added Value — and one measure of Success. Think about your Objectives and what types of Added Value relate back to your desired Rewards and Results — and apply these variables to **THE FORMULA.**

Master The Universe Formula
THE FORMULA = OO + RRR + AA

4. **OO** – Determine your Objectives and Options.
5. **RRR** – Consider potential Results, Reactions, and Rewards to determine your course of action.
6. **AA** – Act and Assess.

PRO TIP: Use the condensed acronym **"ORA"** to remember **THE FORMULA.**

How To MASTER THE UNIVERSE
Personal and Professional Life-Skills Guide

If you want to Master the Universe — follow The Wisdom Way

The Wisdom Way

```
Determine            Consider        Act &
Objectives &   →     Results    →    Assess
Options
                                       │ Learnings
                                       ↓
              Determine            Consider        Act &
              Objectives &   →     Results    →    Assess
              Options
                                                     │ Learnings
                                                     ↓
                                              ⟨ Wisdom ⟩
```

Mastering the Universe is a journey and not a destination. Destinations are endpoints — and endpoints have no future.

Embrace the destinations — and then move on to enjoy the journey.

AFTERWORD

    Breadcrumbs. What kind of breadcrumbs are you going to leave?

Your body is going to die someday. When it does, you will lose access to a major memory storage peripheral — your brain. In fact, your brain's memory storage and information recovery capabilities will likely grow and then diminish over your lifetime.

What if your soul continues after your body passes away? And what if your soul only retains thoughts and emotional feelings — but not the memories stored in your brain? If your soul is fortunate enough to reincarnate into another body, what kind of information and learnings would you like to leave behind for your next incarnation?

Even if you are not reincarnated, or if there is no such thing as reincarnation, what kind of breadcrumbs would you like to leave for your children — or for other people that you care about?

Now is a good time to start journaling or augmenting your memory by documenting learnings that you value the most. This will help reinforce your favorite learnings over time and improve the accuracy of your recall of the learnings. You can periodically review and update your notes to improve the quality of your journey — and share your learnings with others to help improve their journeys through life as well. You can also leave behind contributions such as music, art, buildings, children, protégées, constructive organizations, a better environment, relationships, and good karma.

    What kind of breadcrumbs are you going to leave?

How To MASTER THE UNIVERSE
Personal and Professional Life-Skills Guide

ACKNOWLEDGEMENTS

"There is no such thing as a self-made man."
Arnold Schwarzenegger (1947-), Actor and
California Governor

First, I am grateful for my parents. They were modest income schoolteachers who valued knowledge and integrity over excess wealth.

I have thought about writing a book since my student days at Tulane University. In fact, I designed my triangular "chop," or brand, during my freshman year at Tulane. It includes some Greek symbolism. My theoretical math classes focused more on teaching thinking and problem-solving skills than they did on memorization. Then in my final year at Tulane, I took a graduate level literature course where the grade was primarily based on a final paper to critique my choice of a contemporary writing style that we studied during the semester. Instead of writing a paper "on" a style, I wrote a short story "in" the style I was critiquing. It was a story about a student going to the library to write a paper on the writing style. The student I wrote about critiqued the writing style within the short story. I thought that the professor would either give me an "F" or an "A" for not simply writing a critique. Fortunately, the professor chose the latter and wrote a fun, critique of my short story in the same style — and recommended that I pursue a career in writing. I am very appreciative of the professors and the stimulating learning environment that Tulane University provided.

I spent the next 40 years teaching, consulting, advising, and mostly working on the business leadership side of the technology industry — instead of a career in writing. Even though I was not actively thinking about incorporating these learnings into a book, those years enabled me to acquire the experience and content for the book. I learned from best practices, and I learned from observing mistakes. Thanks to all my business colleagues. And special thanks to Forrest Holleman, my consulting business partner at Global Eyes, LLC — with whom I have shared many discussions regarding the topics in this book.

I still was not serious about writing a book even though my sister and friends had been pushing me to write a book for a long time. Then a couple of years ago a friend from the past, Chihiro Suematsu sent me a note saying, "I have been wanting to express you my gratitude of life, actually." Suematsu-San is a serial author, a Stanford University lecturer, and a Professor at the Kyoto University Graduate School of Business. We used to golf and philosophize over beers during his trips to Stanford — and I had not spoken with him in about twenty years. So, I thanked him and asked him what he meant by that statement. He said "when I was young, hesitating to choose either righteous way or wicked way, I met and saw you and decided to take the former with confidence. It became my foundation of all intellectual, organizational, and social activities." This was a catalyst for me to finally get started on writing a book. Thank you Sis — and thank you, Chihiro Suematsu.

I still did not know whether I wanted to write a fiction or non-fiction book – or what to use as a theme and structure. Then I had an epiphany while practicing yoga with live music at a non-denominational class at Grace Cathedral in San Francisco. The book concept just flowed to me when I was in a semi-conscious meditative mental state. I would structure the book around the Center of the Universe Principle that I had thought up years ago and developed a formula for mastering your life. Thank you, Grace Cathedral, for hosting the yoga sessions.

I initially thought that I could finish the book in about four months, but my wife, Monique encouraged me to take my time writing the book. This extra time has enabled me to do more research on several topics and to refine the book. She also helped reinforce a strong ethical value system over the years. Thank you, Monique, for your support in everything in my life.

ACKNOWLEDGEMENTS

"If you wish to make an apple pie truly from scratch, you must first invent the universe."
Carl Sagan (1934-1996), Astronomer

How To MASTER THE UNIVERSE
Personal and Professional Life-Skills Guide

SAMPLE DISCUSSION POINTS

1. What is an example of when you applied **THE FORMULA** recently? What was the situation? What did you want to accomplish? What were your options? What were the results in terms of reactions or rewards? What did you learn from the situation, and would you act differently next time?
2. What is your favorite breathing technique? How often do you practice it?
3. What is your target identity – to yourself and to others? What habits are you adopting to adapt to that identity?
4. What habit of yours would you like to eliminate? What approach or technique are you going to use to eliminate it? Have you started the habit, and if not, when are you starting?
5. What is a habit that you are trying to develop and for what purpose?
6. Do you plan to apply one of the behavioral modification techniques to yourself or to others? Which techniques?
7. Who have you complimented recently? What did you say and what was the reaction?
8. What is your favorite mantra?
9. How often to you stop to only focus on the attributes and sensations of what you are eating or drinking?
10. What have you done recently that improved your "Karma Pool?"
11. What is a Rule that you have questioned? Did you decide to stay with the rule, ignore, or substitute a different rule? Why and how is it working out?
12. What are you grateful for?

13. Do you think that your mind is more capable than your brain? Is your brain only capable of providing limited access to information and capabilities of your mind? How can you improve your brain's ability to access your mind's capabilities?
14. Does your brain add capabilities to your mind, such as neurological storage of memories or other cognitive abilities? If so, what do you think happens to those memories when your body dies?
15. How does replacing body parts affect your soul? How much of your body can you replace without changing your soul? Do you think that it might be possible to live in a fully artificial body?
16. If we exist in the spiritual world outside of our bodies, are there connections to each other's souls when our bodies are alive. Do they continue to be connected when our bodies die?
17. How do you think that our souls get allocated to specific bodies? Are they naturally allocated, or do they have a choice in the allocation? E.g., If a fetus is aborted, does the soul find another body to inhabit? Are souls allocated to bodies in proximity to other souls with whom they have relationships?
18. Does the increase in population mean that there would be a diluted quality of souls available per body?
19. Do you think there are "old souls" and "young souls?" If so, what are they?
20. Given the historic growth to the current billions of people alive on the planet earth, is there any limitation to the available souls to occupy bodies? What are the souls doing in the meantime?
21. Since the earth is only one of an immeasurable number of potentially inhabitable planets in the galaxy, do you think that souls inhabit bodies adapted to other planets?
22. Does the SOUL-BODY MODEL apply to the Catholic concept of the "Holy Trinity?" The

"Father" being the Cosmos, the "Son" being the body in the physical world, and the "Holy Spirit" being the realm where they intersect?
23. Do you believe in reincarnation? If so, do you believe that talents can follow your soul from one incarnation to another? For example, Mozart and Beethoven appeared to be born with natural musical talents and were child prodigies.
24. Are plagues and natural disasters part of the Cosmos cleansing and regenerating itself just as fires regenerate forests?
25. Who is one of your most respected leaders? Why?
26. In the Negotiations section, there is an anecdote about Sun Microsystems applying P-A-R-T-S techniques to change the game. Which of the techniques did they apply?
27. What is "enough" money for you? Enough for now and for the future?
28. How do you define "Success" for yourself?
29. What topics in the book do you want to research further?
30. What discussion points would you add to this list?

How To MASTER THE UNIVERSE
Personal and Professional Life-Skills Guide

RESOURCES

Augustine, Web. *Inspiring Quotations for Our Times*, 2020

Bander, Richard and Grinder, John. *Frogs into Princes – Neuro Linguistic Programming*. Real People Press. 1979

Brandenburger, Adam M. and Nalebuff, Barry J. *Co-opetition*. Crown Business. 2011

Burgess, Paul. *Natural Born Success, Discover the Instinctive Drives that make you tick*. Wrightbooks. 2007

Carroll, Alan. *The Broadband Connection*, Dallas. Benbella Books, Inc. 2009

Clason, George S. *The Richest Man in Babylon*. Best Success Books. 1926

Clavell, James. *Shogun: The Epic Novel of Japan*. Atheneum. 1975

Coelho, Paulo. *The Alchemist*. Harper Torch (1993 English edition). 1988 (original)

Covy, Stephen R. *The 7 Habits of Highly Effective People*. New York: Simon and Schuster, 1989

Descartes, Rene. *Proofs of God's Existence*, 1596-1650

Dictionary.com

Drucker, Peter. *The Practice of Management*: HarperCollins Publishers. 2010

Gibran, Kahlil. *The Prophet*. New York. Penguin Classics, 1919

Gladwell, Malcom. *Tipping Point: How Little Things Can Make a Big Difference*. Little, Brown, and Company. 2006

Gladwell, Malcom. *Blink: The Power of Thinking Without Thinking*. Back Bay Books. 2007

Hanh, Thich Nhat. *Living Buddha, Living Christ*. Riverhead, 1995

Hanh, Thich Nhat. *The Miracle of Mindfulness*. Beacon Press, 1996

Harari, Yuval Noah. *Sapiens: A Brief History of Humankind*. Harper, 2015

Harari, Yuval Noah. *Homo Deus: A brief History of Tomorrow*. Signal, 2016

Harari, Yuval Noah. *21 Lessons for the 21st Century*. Spiegel & Grau, 2018

Henley, William Ernest. *Invictus*, 1875 (published in Book of Verses, 1888)

Hersey, P. and Blanchard, K. H.: *Management of Organizational Behavior – Utilizing Human Resources*, New Jersey/Prentice Hall, 1969

Iliff, Jeff. *One more reason to get a good night's sleep*: TEDMED 2014

Kahneman, Daniel. *Thinking, Fast and Slow*. Farrar, Straus, and Giroux, 2013

Lakhiani, Vishen. *The Code of the Extraordinary Mind*. Rodale Books, 2019

Moore, Geoffrey. *Crossing the Chasm*. HarperCollins, 2014

Musashi, Miyamoto. *The Book of Five Rings*. 1645

Nestor, James. *Breath: The New Science of a Lost Art*. Riverhead, 2020

Robbins, Anthony. *Unlimited Power*. New York: Fawcett-Columbine Publishers, 1986

Sherwood, Ben. *The Survivors Club: The Secrets and Science that Could Save Your Life*. Grand Central Publishing, 2009

Siebel, Thomas and Malone, Michael. *Virtual Selling: Going Beyond the Automated Sales Force to Achieve Total Sales Quality*, Diane Pub Co, 1996

Suzuki, Wendy. *The brain-changing benefits of exercise*. TEDWomen 2017

Rackham, Neil. *Spin Selling*, McGraw-Hill, 1988

Toffler, Alvin. *Powershift: Knowledge, Wealth, and Violence at the Edge of the 21st Century*. Mass Market Paperback, 1991

Tzu, Sun. *The Art of War*. Approximately 5th Century BC Wikipedia

ABOUT THE AUTHOR

Tad Bogdan was born and spent his pre-teen years in rural Ohio where he augmented the influence of mid-west values of integrity and hard work, with an interest in yoga and meditation. He enjoyed a teenage life in Florida until moving to New Orleans to study theoretical mathematics, philosophy, and business administration at Tulane University. He started his professional life as a math teacher and wrestling coach before transitioning into a business career and moving to the San Francisco Bay Area. Tad launched several market-leading business initiatives and was the CEO of multiple technology companies. Throughout his career, he integrated his passion for human development into professional training, coaching, and mentoring roles. He has served on several Boards of Directors and Advisors, including the Board of Advisors for the School of Science and Engineering at Tulane University. Tad is currently a speaker and consultant for topics related to this book.

www.ingramcontent.com/pod-product-compliance
Lightning Source LLC
Chambersburg PA
CBHW071356210526
45465CB00001B/113